Suryavamshi

Suryavamshi

The Sun Kings of Rajasthan

Abanindranath Tagore

Translated and adapted by
Sandipan Deb

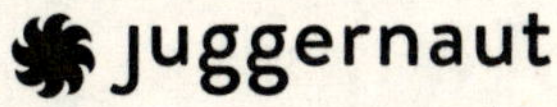

JUGGERNAUT BOOKS
C-I-128, First Floor, Sangam Vihar, Near Holi Chowk,
New Delhi 110080, India

Originally published in 1905 in Bengali as *Raj Kahini*
written by Abanindranath Tagore
First published by Juggernaut Books 2024

10 9 8 7 6 5 4 3 2 1

P-ISBN: 9789353456436
E-ISBN: 9789353455897

Typeset in Adobe Caslon Pro by R. Ajith Kumar, Noida

Printed at Replika Press Pvt. Ltd.

To Ma,

who has devoted her life to worrying about me

Contents

Introduction

Abanindranath Tagore (1871–1951), affectionately called Aban Thakur by Bengalis, was an extraordinary talent, though he was obviously much overshadowed by his uncle, Rabindranath Tagore. In the early twentieth century, he and his elder brother, Gaganendranath, created the first modern Indian art movement. The Bengal School of Art broke away from Western traditions and sought beauty, freedom and inspiration in India's own artistic heritage.

Abanindranath also wrote several books, principally for children and teenagers, but they are classic works that anyone of any age can enjoy and mull over too. His tales brim over with the visual imagination of a master painter. In fact, in his children's novel *Buro Angla,* he describes himself as a man who 'writes pictures'.

The stories of *Raj Kahini*, which we have titled *Suryavamshi*, are adapted from – or rather, inspired by – *The Annals and Antiquities of Rajasthan* by Lieutenant Colonel James Tod (1782–1835), an East India Company soldier and amateur anthropologist and historian. Tod's account of Rajasthan's history and demographics was based on folklore, the race memory of the people of the land and his own diligent research.

Unless they are pursuing a PhD in the social and political history of Rajasthan, most readers today are likely to find *Annals and Antiquities* a boring tome. But Abanindranath picked out a few stories from it featuring the kings of the state of Mewar who were from the Suryavamsha – Dynasty of the Sun – and turned them into stunning word paintings. Light and shadow, and colours and changes of season, are ever present in his work. Fortresses perch on mountains like hovering banks of clouds, cavalries turn day into night with the dust stirred up by their charging horses, and a shrine inside a mountain cave appears drenched in blood in the fading sunlight.

The stories variously tell of love, sacrifice, jealousy, courage, greed and treachery . . . emotions and traits that define the human condition. Over every story hangs the shadow of violence, war and often senseless slaughter. Almost all the heroes are deeply flawed human beings or, reminiscent of classical Greek tragedy, captives of destinies over which they have little control.

Raj Kahini has been staple literary diet for generations of Bengalis. Translating Abanindranath's exceptional word imagery and the underlying themes for a wider audience – and a twenty-first-century one – has been a challenging task.

Many of the stories, especially the earlier ones, emerge out of the mists of legend, transmitted over the centuries by poets and travelling minstrels. Some of the later narratives too may have various versions, due to the fact that most of this is oral history carried down and altered and embellished over time. Tod recorded the most prevalent versions and Abanindranath brought his own extraordinary imagination to bear on them. Mapping the exact facts and their timelines is a complex task best left to ethno-historians and archaeologists.

The first story in *Raj Kahini* is about Shiladitya, supposedly the boon-child of Suryadev, the Sun God, and founder of the Mewar Suryavamshi dynasty. The last is set in the sixteenth century and is about the ascent of Rana Sanga, the one-eyed warrior who would fight Babur and lose to him in 1527 in the battle of Khanwa. More than the battle of Panipat, this would mark the beginning of the Mughal era. Sanga was the last independent Hindu king who ruled over a very large territory in northern India.

These tales were collected by Tod in the early nineteenth century. Abanindranath, in turn, rewrote Tod's *Annals* in the early twentieth century, and you are reading the stories from Aban Thakur's book in the twenty-first century.

Today we know some of the characters who appear here by names that are different from what they are in *Raj Kahini*. Bappaditya, who was the first Suryavamshi to sit on the throne of Mewar, is now referred to as Bappa Rawal. Jaimull, brother of Sangramsingh – Sanga – was actually Jagmull. Sanga was the youngest of three brothers, not the eldest.

Names of places too may have changed or some villages and towns may have disappeared. I have let all the names be as they are. I have not tried to correct the factual inaccuracies in the tales other than take care of a few obvious logical inconsistencies.

My reasoning for this is that Abanindranath was not trying to write 'history' as understood in academia, just as the tales of King Arthur and his Round Table did not come down through the ages as 'history'. It is also important to remember that Abanindranath wrote this book during the first flush of the Indian struggle for freedom from colonialism. His art played a key role in the revival of Indian pride. In 1905, soon after Lord Curzon announced the Partition of Bengal on communal lines, Abanindranath painted the first and still-iconic depiction of Bharat Mata. *Raj Kahini* was thus part of a bigger national project. However, Abanindranath refused to give his heroes a halo and their lives fictitious happy endings. He remained true to the basic plot lines that Tod had noted down while adding a rich layer of an artist's notion of what those times would have been like and how those men and women would have lived, thought and fought.

Abanindranath's book belongs firmly to the tradition of itihasa, the uniquely Indic concept that straddles history and mythology and tries to convey a truth that goes beyond dry facts and statistics.

1

Shiladitya

Once upon a time, in the days before Shiladitya was born, when the last king of Raja Kanaksen's dynasty was still ruling Ballavipur, there stood a huge temple dedicated to Suryadev, the Sun God, next to a sacred lake called Suryakund – the lake of Suryadev.

A very old priest lived there. He had no children or friends. Like the sun, alone in the infinite sky, the noble priest was a lonely being in that sun temple on the banks of the vast sacred lake, whose waters were as blue as the heavens above. The priest did everything himself – lighting the lamps in the temple, ringing the giant bell and performing the daily rituals at dawn and dusk. He had no servants, no followers and no disciples.

At daybreak and at twilight every day, the old Brahmin would perform the aarti dedicated to the god in the temple with a brass lamp that weighed thirty seers (roughly 30 kg). Every day the temple bell, as huge as the crown of a demon king, would be rung by his lean hand. 'If I could get a companion,' he would think, 'I could leave all these responsibilities to that person and die in peace.'

The god fulfilled his devotee's wish. One evening, early in the winter month of Paush, when the sun had set and a dark fog obscured the world, the priest was locking the temple's iron doors, as massive as the breast armour of the mighty Bhima. An ashen-faced Brahmin girl appeared before him – dressed in rags but very beautiful. It was as if the evening star, scared of the cold, was seeking refuge in the temple of Suryadev. The old man noticed that the girl, dressed in a widow's garment, appeared to be well born.

'Who are you? What do you want?' he asked. The girl put her two small lotus petal-like hands together and said: 'Lord, I ask for shelter. I am the only daughter of Devaditya, the Vedic scholar in the land of the Gurjars. My name is Subhaga, the lucky one. But I was widowed on the night of my wedding and my husband's family threw me out as they believed that I had brought them ill luck. Lord, I had a mother, but she is no more now, please give me shelter.'

'My dear orphan,' said the priest. 'What happy home can you expect here? I have neither food nor garments. I am very poor and have no friends.'

But even as the priest spoke these words a voice inside his head was telling him: 'You poor lonely man, make this girl your friend, give her shelter.'

Let me give her a home, he thought. *For eighty years I have worshipped the Sun God alone; now, at the end of my life, maybe I can leave that responsibility to this unfortunate girl.*

Still, he hesitated. And then, suddenly, a single ray of the sun from the western sky pierced through the evening dark and fell on the desolate girl's face. It was as if Suryadev were speaking directly to the priest – 'Accept her, my dearest devotee. I have chosen this poor widowed girl to be in my service all her life.'

The priest bowed to his god and offered shelter in the Temple of the Sun to the daughter of Devaditya.

Years passed. Subhaga learnt all the temple tasks, but her soft, delicate hands could never manage to lift the thirty-seer lamp. So the old priest continued to perform the twice-daily aartis.

One day, Subhaga noticed that the priest's frail body seemed to have reached its limits – the lamp was shaking in his hands. She went to the market at Ballavipur and bought a small lamp that weighed just one seer. 'Father, please use this to do your aarti to Suryadev this evening,' she told the priest. He smiled and said: 'The evening aarti has to be done with the same lamp that was used in the morning. Keep it. I will use the new lamp tomorrow, a new day.'

The next day, at noon, as the sun's light flooded the earth, the priest taught Subhaga the holiest of all mantras to the Sun God. Suryadev himself would appear before his devotee when the mantra was uttered, but it could be used only once; a second utterance meant certain death. Then, as evening turned to night and the glow of the aarti lamp dimmed, the light of the priest's life died softly. The sun sank, plunging the world in darkness. Subhaga was left all alone in the world.

She spent the first few days weeping over her loss. Then, one morning, she began clearing up the jungle around the temple and planting fruit trees and flowering plants. Many more days went by in cleaning the temple's stone walls and painting leaves, flowers, birds, elephants and scenes from the Puranas and itihasa on them. Finally, Subhaga had nothing more to do. She would roam around in her orchard and among her flower beds. In some time, a few fruits started to ripen, a few flowers bloomed, and a few birds, colourful butterflies and a gaggle of children appeared.

The butterflies were happy with a little bit of nectar from the flowers, and the birds with pecking at one or two ripe fruits. The gang of naughty boys, however, would tear off the flowers, pluck the fruits and break the boughs of the trees. But Subhaga never scolded them and tolerated their mischief cheerfully. On the green grass under the trees, the little children would place their many-hued mats and play. And thus passed Subhaga's days.

The monsoon arrived with its black clouds, flashes of lightning and rumble of thunder. One day, a whistling razor-sharp eastern wind sliced the stems of Subhaga's flowering plants, tore off the leaves from her trees and nearly laid waste her beloved garden. The birds were blown away, the broken wings of the butterflies littered the earth like the petals of flowers, and the children disappeared.

As the rains raged, Subhaga sat alone and mourned over the memories of her parents, the cruelty of her in-laws, and her husband's smiling, handsome face on their wedding night. And she kept thinking – 'How will I spend all my life in this friendless foreign land?' Her eyes, as black and beautiful as a deer's, welled up.

She looked towards the east and saw darkness; towards the west, and it was dark there too; then towards the north and the south . . . which were also dark. It was dark all around. She remembered that it was on a day of blackness like this that she had come to the temple. Tonight too was just as dismal – the same stormy wind, the same huge, empty Temple of the Sun. But there was no kindly old man who had given refuge to an ill-fated orphan girl. Subhaga's tears fell in the dark like raindrops.

She shut all the doors to the temple, lit the lamp and did her aarti. And then, for some unknown reason, she sat down to meditate before the idol of the lord. As the minutes passed, her eyes became still – the shrieking of the storm and the crashing of thunder seemed to move far, far away. Subhaga no longer felt any sorrow or grief. It was as if the intensity of the sun had shredded the dark night that had enveloped her soul.

Slowly, fearfully, Subhaga uttered the mantra the priest had taught her. And the whole world seemed to shudder and wake up. She seemed surrounded by birdsong, melodious tunes from a flute and a joyous hubbub. Then, with a deep rumbling that shook the skies, bathing the world in glorious light, as if melting the stone walls and the iron gates of the temple,

Suryadev, the Sun God – brighter than a billion blazing fires – appeared before Subhaga on a chariot drawn by seven emerald horses.

No human eye could stand such dazzling light. Subhaga covered her face with her hands and said: 'O Lord, save me, forgive me, the whole world burns!'

'Do not fear, girl,' said the god. 'Ask for your boon.' As he spoke, his radiance decreased and only a warm reddish glow remained on Subhaga's head, like the streak of vermilion along the parting of a married woman's hair. Subhaga said: 'Lord, I have no husband or children, I am but a widow all alone. Grant me this boon that I no longer have to stay on this earth. Let me die today at your feet, rid of all pain and anguish.'

Said Suryadev: 'Girl, gods cannot boon death. That can only be their curse. Ask me for a boon.' Then Subhaga lay herself down before him and said: 'Lord, if you have to grant me a boon, give me a son and a daughter. Let me nurture them. Let the son be as bright as you are and let the daughter be as beautiful as a moonbeam.'

It shall be so, said the Sun God, and vanished. Subhaga was slowly overcome by sleep and lay down on the stone floor. Outside, a downpour started again. As day broke, in her slumber, she seemed to hear two birds singing a wondrous tune in her ruined garden. When the golden rays of dawn fell on her eyelids, she got up hurriedly and felt a tug at her dress.

Two little babies were sleeping next to her. Suryadev had granted her wish. The children looked as beautiful as the gods themselves. Because they had been born in the huge, empty temple, hidden from human eyes, she named them Gayab and Gayabi – the invisible ones.

Clutching Gayab and Gayabi to her breast, Subhaga walked out to her garden. The sun was rising in the east and the moon setting in the west. She saw the sun light up Gayab's face and the moonbeams sink slowly into Gayabi's black hair. But Subhaga's heart quaked at that sight. Something told her that it would not be possible to keep Gayabi on this earth for long.

The children grew up. Gayab began to go to school, and Gayabi started learning the work of the temple from her mother. Gayab was restless and naughty, and Gayabi quiet and obedient. Many children would come to the temple to play with Gayabi, but Gayab's mischiefs would drive the other boys to their wits' end. Finally, all of them got together and decided that Gayab was better than them, both in studies and in physical strength, so they would make him king and they would be his subjects. Then he would not be able to give them such a hard time. And they lifted Gayab on to their shoulders and danced.

Gayab was up there, very happy, when a little boy said: 'I am the king's head priest. I will chant the required mantras and coronate him with the royal tilak.' The boys put Gayab down on a small mound of earth. Gayab was sitting there like a king on his throne, and one of them put the red mark on his forehead and asked: 'Gayab, we know your name, but tell us your mother's name and your father's.' Gayab said: 'My name is Gayab, my sister's name is Gayabi. My mother's name is Subhaga. My father's name – what is my father's name?' He did not know that he was the Sun God's boon-child.

The boys now laughed and jeered at him. Overwhelmed with shame, Gayab kicked down the mound that had been his throne, slapped and punched his mates in their already swollen and bruised faces and ran back to the temple, trembling with rage.

Subhaga was teaching Gayabi how to do the god's aarti with a small brass lamp. Gayab rushed in, snatched it from her hand and threw it with all his strength. The lamp rang against the stone wall and broke into pieces. A stone with Suryadev's image on it fell down on the floor. 'What have you done, you lunatic?' said Subhaga.

'You have spoiled the holy aarti and insulted the Sun God!'

'I know neither the sun nor the god,' said Gayab. 'Tell me, who is my father? Or I'll throw the idol into the lake.' And though even Bhima, the most powerful of all men ever born, could not have lifted the great idol, Subhaga, seeing Gayab's fury, was afraid at the thought of what he might be capable of doing. She grabbed his hands and said: 'Calm down, dearest, please calm down, don't insult the Sun God any more. Why do you want to know your father's name? I am your mother, Gayabi is your sister, what more do you need?'

Gayab burst into tears. 'Then what am I, Mother – a mean, despicable, unholy piece of dirt, lowlier than the worst beggar?' The words pierced Subhaga's heart like deadly arrows. She sat down, her hands over her face. *Oh Lord, what have you done?* she pleaded silently. *How do I explain it all to this unruly child, how do I comfort him? Gayab and Gayabi are not mean, not unholy; they are the son and daughter of Suryadev himself, holier than all others.*

She thought of the sacred Surya mantra, but when she recalled that uttering it a second time would mean her death, and her children would be orphaned, she could not bear to do it. 'Dearest, stop, let it be, let us go away somewhere,' she said. 'And please know that Suryadev the Sun God himself is your father.'

Gayab shook his head; he would not believe her. So a helpless Subhaga said: 'Then shut all the doors of the temple. You will be able to see your father now, but you will lose me forever.' Her eyes filled with tears. 'Why do you torture our Ma?' Gayabi asked. Gayab did not answer; he shut all the doors.

Subhaga took her children's hands into hers and sat down in front of the idol to meditate. Once, desolate, she had uttered the mantra without fear when she wanted to die, but today, agony and dread coiled around her heart like poisonous snakes.

Soon, Suryadev manifested himself in his terrifying form, as if drenching the entire temple in a cascade of blood. Subhaga said: 'Lord, who is the father of Gayab and Gayabi?' The Sun God remained silent. Within moments his terrible heat burned his poor devotee Subhaga's body to ashes.

'Ma! Ma!' cried out Gayabi.

'Where is Ma?' shouted Gayab.

The Sun God did not reply; he merely pointed to the heap of ashes on the stone floor.

Gayab realized that his mother was no more. His eyes blazing with pain and rage, he picked up the stone with Suryadev's image on it and flung it at the god. It struck the god's crown and bounced off, like a piece of flaming coal. Gayab fell to the floor, unconscious.

When he regained his senses the god had disappeared and Gayabi was sitting by him. 'Where is the Sun God?' asked Gayab. Gayabi pointed at the black rock and said: 'Take this. This is the Adityashila, the sun-stone. Whoever you drop this on will die. Suryadev has given this to you, saying that you are his son. From today your name is Shiladitya, after this stone. Your dynasty will be called the 'Suryavamsha'. Your children, the Suryavamshis, will rule the earth. And whenever you call for it, the seven-horsed chariot of the Sun God will rise from the Suryakund lake and come to you. Go, ride that chariot with the sun-stone in your hand and conquer the world.'

'But what do I do about you?' asked Gayab. 'Leave me here in the temple,' said Gayabi. 'I will live on the fruits of the orchard and the water from the lake. When you become king, come back and take me to your royal palace.'

A very happy Gayab left his sister and rode off in the seven-horsed chariot to conquer the world. Gayabi immersed Subhaga's ashes in the lake and dropped to the stone floor, weeping over the loss of her mother and brother.

Late that night, when there were no stars in the sky and not a glimmer of light on earth, the temple suddenly shook and shuddered with a terrible noise. And then, half of it sank into the ground, taking with it the idol of Suryadev that weighed many tonnes, and Gayabi, as beautiful as the most exquisite doll. Terrified, she tried to escape, but it was of no avail. She tried climbing up the wall, but it was smooth as glass and offered no grip for her fingers and toes. She called out her brother's name and lost consciousness. Then it was all over, all became dark.

Years passed. Shiladitya, riding his seven-horsed chariot, roamed the world, raising armies from near and far and conquering many lands. Finally he returned to Ballavipur. Using the sun-stone, he defeated and killed the king of Ballavipur in a face-to-face combat, ascended the throne, appointed some of his schoolmates as ministers, some others as army commanders, and got rid of all the useless old officials. He then married

Pushpavati, the princess of Chandravati, in a splendid ceremony, after which he returned to rest in his bedroom made of the purest marble.

The night lengthened and there was silence all around. The servant girl who had been fanning him was dozing off and the flame of the golden lamp near his head had begun to flicker. Shiladitya saw his sister Gayabi's innocent face in a dream. She seemed to be looking at him from a great distance, and someone from the direction of the temple of Suryadev was calling out his name.

Shiladitya woke up with a scream. Dawn had broken. He quickly gathered some soldiers, climbed on to his royal chariot and rode to the temple. The doors of the temple, like the two plates of Bhima's breast armour, were shut tight. Creepers had grown around them over the years, fastening them tight like chains of steel. Shiladitya removed the foliage with his own hands and opened the doors. As sunlight burst into the temple, a swarm of startled bats flew out. Shiladitya went in. The spot where the idol had stood was cloaked in darkness, as if a pitch-black curtain had been drawn over it.

'Gayabi, Gayabi, where are you?' called out Shiladitya.

'Poor Gayabi, where is Gayabi?' the darkness replied.

Shiladitya ordered some torches to be brought in.

In their flaming light he saw that the northern side of the temple, with the idol, had descended into the earth. Only the black stone heads of the seven horses were above the ground, splayed like the many hoods of a giant mythical serpent. There was no trace of the room where Shiladitya used to play with Gayabi, the room where, after a day's play, he and his sister would go to sleep, listening to their mother's bedtime tales of the land of the Gurjars; or of the room where the great brass lamp had stood like a deodar tree.

Shiladitya stood at the edge of the vast abyss and cried, 'Gayabi! Gayabi!' His desperate pleas spun around the chasm and were soon lost in the black world beneath.

Shiladitya sighed. There was nothing that he, the great king, could do. He returned in silence to his palace.

Later that day, on his command, workers began to wrap the entire temple in thick gold foil. The king did not place any new idol in the Temple of the Sun. The horses remained as they were, half awake at the mouth of the void. Then Shiladitya extracted marble from the mountains around and built a marvellous platform around the temple. Whenever there was a war, he would meditate on the banks of the Suryakund lake and the seven-horsed chariot would rise from its waters. Whenever he went to battle in it, he won.

But in the end, one of his ministers, a man whom he had loved and trusted the most, betrayed him. He had been the only person other than Shiladitya who knew where the chariot came from. When the Parad barbarians from the land of Shyamnagar from across the Sindhu river attacked Ballavipur, this traitor, in exchange for a few gold coins, desecrated the water of the lake with the blood of a cow.

On the morning of the day of battle with those barbarians, when Shiladitya prayed to the Sun God on the banks of the lake, the heavenly chariot did not appear. The king kept calling out the names of the seven horses, but the water did not stir.

A dismayed Shiladitya rode out in his royal chariot to face the enemy and was killed. At the end of the full day of battle, as the sun sank over the horizon, so did Suryadev's boon-child. The victorious barbarians destroyed the golden Temple of the Sun and left Ballavipur in ruins.

2

Goha

Nestled among the mighty Vindhya mountains that touch the skies, the marble palace of the kings of Chandravati was as pretty and pleasant as a small leaf-covered bird's nest in a grove of giant banyan trees. Some days before his battle with the barbarians, Shiladitya had sent his wife Pushpavati, the princess of Chandravati, accompanied by a few valiant Rajputs, to stay with her parents in this palace. Pushpavati was then with child.

Shiladitya had dearly hoped that after the battle he would spend the winter with Pushpavati resting in the palace in the Vindhyas. Then, after Pushpavati gave birth to their child, they would return to Ballavipur with the newborn. But the Almighty had doused those dreams. A poisoned arrow shot by a barbarian enemy had pierced both Shiladitya's heart and all its desires. He lost his life on the battlefield. His beloved wife Pushpavati was left lost and lonesome in that magnificent mountain palace.

Fifty yards beneath Pushpavati's bedroom in the mountain palace ran the highway to Ballavipur. After arriving in Chandravati, she had got built a small marble deck set into the sheer mountain wall at a height of about twenty-five yards, as if floating in space. Every day the young queen would sit there, gazing at the highway from time to time while she sewed an image of Suryadev in his seven-horsed chariot on a silver fabric using a gold needle and fine green silk yarn. And she dreamed of tying this feather-light turban on the king's head when he returned from battle. They would then rest on that deck hewed into the rock face like a slice of shimmering cloud, and she would listen to the king's tales about the war.

Sometimes Pushpavati would glimpse the light glinting off the head of a spear far away on the highway from Ballavipur. Then the emissary from Ballavipur would ride up on his black stallion, plant his javelin on the ground, bow to Queen Pushpavati sitting in her veranda and speed away like an arrow towards the portals of the royal palace.

On the days when the servant girl brought her a letter from Shiladitya, Pushpavati would let all her tasks wait and sit on the deck that hung in the sky with the precious message clutched in her hands.

On those happy days, when an elderly Jat, singing as he made his way to his fields, or a shepherd boy grazing his goats under the mountains, bowed to her till his forehead touched the ground, Pushpavati would drop into his hands a string of emeralds, or perhaps an anklet of gold.

The loyal subjects would hold the queen's gift to their foreheads and bless her a thousand times before going on their way. At sunset, the emissary would ride back to Ballavipur on his black horse with Pushpavati's letter to Shiladitya, spear in hand.

For quite a long time after he left, the princess would hear the clatter of the black horse's hooves as they echoed off the mountains in the silent twilight. Sometimes an old Jat's earthy song or a sweet melody from a shepherd's flute would waft in on the evening breeze. Then the bells would ring out deep for the evening puja at the mountaintop temple of Ma Bhavani, the goddess whose home is the Vindhyas. Pushpavati would hide the king's letter in her hair as she swirled it into a bun, wear the ordained silk saree and sit down for her puja to the devi.

'O Ma Chamunde, O Ma Bhavani, please bring the king back healthy and victorious from his war,' she would pray. 'O Bhagvati, may the son who is born to me be as luminous as the king, and may he love his own queen as much as my king loves me.'

Alas, not all the wishes of humans are fulfilled! Pushpavati's son would shine as bright as his father, but that dream she had – of listening to tales of the war from her king as they rested on their marble perch, and of wrapping the king's head with the subtle-as-air turban that she was embroidering – were never realized. Her dreams remained dreams; she never met her king and husband again in this life.

The day Shiladitya died on the Ballavipur battlefield, Pushpavati was sitting with her mother in the royal palace of Chandravati, working away on the delicate silver cloth. The work was almost done; all that remained was to embroider Shiladitya's name at the feet of the image of Suryadev she had sewn.

With great care, Pushpavati had just pierced the cloth with her gold needle – finer than her night-black hair and brighter than a flame – when it pricked, like the sting of a wasp, her finger which was soft as the petal of a champa flower. Her eyes welled up in pain. She saw a drop of her blood glittering like a crimson gemstone on the silver fabric that had been as unblemished as moonlight till then. Quickly, she tried to clean up the bloodstain with the purest water. But once the water was sprinkled on the stain, that one drop kept spreading and stained the whole of the fine cloth, just as the faint scent of a flower can make all the air around redolent.

As she watched that bloodstain grow, Pushpavati's soul cried out. She looked at her mother with tearful eyes and said: 'Ma, bid me farewell, I must return to Ballavipur. My heart is anxious, who knows what calamity has struck there.' Her worried mother said, 'Stay for a few more days, girl. Let the child be born.'

'No, no, no, Ma!' cried Pushpavati.

That evening a small palanquin, covered in blue silk and carried between two camel-backs, guarded by eighty valiant Rajput warriors, started off on the road to Ballavipur. Pushpavati had bidden farewell to Chandravati, leaving the palace and the kingdom desolate.

To reach Ballavipur from Chandravati, a great desert had to be crossed. The highway extended from Chandravati to Veernagar at the foot of the Malia mountains, after which the only way one could reach Ballavipur was by camel, through the fire-hot sand. It was when Pushpavati arrived at the end of the road and stood facing the sands that she learnt Shiladitya was no more. The barbarians had razed Ballavipur to the ground.

Not a tear dropped from her eyes, not a word escaped her lips, but her heart felt as barren as the endless desert that stretched before her. She threw her priceless jewels into the yellow dust and wiped the vermilion off her forehead. Then, donning the garment of a widow, Pushpavati, the beloved queen of King Shiladitya, took shelter as a sanyasin in a vast cave in the Malia mountains.

When ten months and ten days were over, a prince was born to the hermit queen in the dark grotto beyond the desert. He was given the name Goha.

On that very day, Pushpavati called for her dearest childhood playmate, Kamalavati, who lived in Veernagar. Then, in the presence of the eighty loyal Rajput warriors, she handed over the infant prince to Kamalavati. 'My friend, I bequeath Goha to you,' she said. 'Please bring him up as a mother would a son. What can I tell you, my sister? Please see that no one neglects the prince. And when my body becomes ash from the flames, do pour a handful of that ash into the Ganga on the full moon night of the month of Kartik and pray that I will not be widowed in my next life.' Tears drenched Kamalavati's cheeks.

That evening, the eighty faithful warriors lit a pyre of fragrant sandalwood and stood in a circle around it. Pushpavati, wife of Shiladitya and his resolute partner, queen of the Rajputs and sanyasin, plunged into the roaring flames with a smile on her lips. Soon her blossom-like body turned into ash and all around the fire the cry went up: 'Hail the great queen! Hail the steadfast goddess!'

With Goha asleep in her arms and a fistful of ash, Kamalavati returned to Veernagar, wiping her tears. And the eighty braves too came with her and settled in Veernagar to form a protective shell around their beloved prince.

The queen of Chandravati tried often to take her grandson back with her, but the eighty warriors from Ballavipur would not let Goha go. 'Our queen bequeathed our prince to us,' they would say. 'We will look after him. Let the prince stay in this desert and be the king of the Rajputs of Ballavipur. This is his royal abode.'

So, Goha grew up in Kamalavati's home in Veernagar.

Kamalavati, being a Brahmin, tried to make Goha a scholar of the shastras, but this son of a warrior-king was not interested in studies. He would spend his time in the forests and mountains, sometimes with the Bhil adivasi people as one of their own, and sometimes with the Rajput soldiers as their king. Sometimes he would go off on horseback to hunt lions or with a net on his shoulders to track down and catch deer.

Veernagar lay at the foot of the Malia mountains. Its denizens were quiet, peaceable and gentle souls. But high up in the mountains, where tigers rumbled and roamed, deer grazed, serpents hissed in the darkness, waterfalls burbled day and night, and where the air was ripe with the scent of mysterious flowers and the trees cast giant shadows, there in the jungles where it was always dusk lived Mandlik, the king of the Bhils. He was dark as a snake, strong as a tiger, majestic as a lion, but truthful, trustworthy and simple as a child.

One day, Goha, with his Bhil friends, rode up to the kingdom on his horse. There, thousands of Bhil boys, dressed in tiger skin and with spear in hand, crowded around the prince, beat their drums and went dancing from door to door, shouting: 'Our king has arrived! The king has come!' Soon they reached the royal abode. Mandlik, the elderly king of the Bhils, came out of his thatch-roofed house and asked: 'Hey boys, where is he, your new king?' The boys pointed at Goha.

The old Bhil's eyes studied Goha for a long time. Then he said: 'This is all good, so now put a tilak on the new king.' A Bhil boy cut one of his fingers and drew the royal tilak with blood on Goha's forehead while King Mandlik watched. Under Bhil law, no one was allowed to ever wipe that tilak off.

Now that Goha was a real king, he sat in the royal court, on a small, low stool at the feet of the elderly king. No one had sat there for a long time because Mandlik did not have any children. His subjects may have been poor and struggling, but their panther-like sons lit up their homes. Yet the king's home had always been dark and empty. Now, when Goha with his royal tilak sat on his stool before the entire Bhil community, the aged Mandlik's eyes brimmed with joy as he looked at the young prince.

The Bhil king had a younger brother. A decade earlier, they had had a great fight over something and had severed ties with each other. But the day Goha was anointed, the younger brother suddenly came down from the Himalayas to the Bhil kingdom – to find that the son of a Rajput had captured the post of crown prince.

The royal court was in session. Burning with rage, the Bhil king's younger brother barged in and asked Mandlik: 'O brother! With age, have you totally lost your senses? A father's kingdom comes to the son. You could not produce a son, so I should be king when you die. What on earth is your logic of putting a Rajput boy on the Bhil crown prince's stool?'

'Brother, calm down,' said Mandlik.

'I will calm down the day I burn you on the pyre,' said the brother, and left, panting in fury.

'Be gone!' said the Bhil king. 'From this day you are my enemy.' He then sat on his throne with Goha on his lap and got all the Bhil leaders to pledge, placing their hands on the boy's forehead, that in good times and bad, in times of trouble and peril, they would defend Goha, and Goha's enemies would be their enemies too.

Then the court was dismissed. After some fun and frolic, Goha returned to Veernagar.

But that night, while the world slept, Mandlik came stealthily to Goha and told him: 'Goha, I love you like a son. I have made you king. Give me your dagger so that I can kill your foes with my own hands.' From his waistband, Goha took out the lethally sharp dagger with his name carved on the hilt and gave it to Mandlik.

The Bhil king stepped out, dagger in hand. Fireflies glowed on the mountain wall; the cicadas were chirping and one could hear the tigers roar in their faraway lairs. It was the dead of night. The Bhil king knocked on his brother's door. There was no answer. Quietly, Mandlik entered the house. He saw his brother asleep on the floor, like any common Bhil, one hand covering his face.

Suddenly, Mandlik seemed to feel a great blow to his heart. He looked down at his handsome brother, a statue sculpted from the blackest of stones, lying on the floor, and he could not hold back his tears. *How cruel I am!* he thought. *I gave away my brother's kingdom to an outsider, and now I think of him as an enemy who must be killed in his sleep!*

The king sat down on the floor near the head of the twenty-year-old prince and called out: 'Brother!' He called once, he called again, he removed his brother's perfectly shaped hand from his face and called out: 'Dear brother!' He received no reply.

Then the old king brought his face down, close to his brother's, his fingers playing with his curly hair, and asked: 'Are you angry with me, brother? Will you not speak to me? I shall conquer half of the Himalayas for you, I shall make you king there. Please get up, speak to me. My dearest brother, why did you leave me and spend the last ten years wandering around in the mountains? Why couldn't you stay safe, under my eyes? Do you think I ever wanted to love that Rajput boy? After you left, I was all alone. And then Goha came and lit up my barren home. My brother, please get up now,

I have given away your kingdom, and then came to kill you as an enemy, please take this dagger – plunge it in my heart, and all problems will be resolved.'

Mandlik thrust the dagger into his brother's hand, but the sharp knife slid down from his clutch. The old king was startled. His brother's body seemed rather cold. He put his ear to his heart and could hear nothing. 'Brother! Brother!' he screamed.

All his anger was now directed at Goha. If Goha had not been there, he could have brought his younger brother back to his bosom after ten long years. Would the Bhil prince have then died from grief and a broken heart over his lost kingdom? For a long time, Mandlik sat caressing his brother's chest. But alas, just as a bird escapes its cage, the life spirit had taken flight a long time ago, leaving the young Bhil's handsome body an empty shell.

Mandlik could not sit in that room any longer. He opened the doors of the house and stood outside under the night sky with the dagger in his hand. His whole inner self seemed to be crying out: 'Goha, what have you done? You took my kingdom, you took my throne, you tore the two brothers apart. Goha, have you finally become my enemy?'

Then, suddenly, two Bhil girls walked by on the

mountain path, their arms around each other. One was saying: 'Have you seen how good-looking the king is?' And the other: 'When the new king held my hand and danced with me, his face seemed to me to be like the moon at its most beautiful.'

Mandlik sighed. His subjects were already discarding him as if he were some old, tattered rag, he thought. He had no one in the world that he could call his own.

His heart and mind blank, he kept staring at the huge full moon. At that point two Rajput soldiers on black horses passed. One said: 'Mate, on this auspicious day, why did our prince sit on the crown prince's stool and not on the throne of the Bhil kingdom?' The other replied: 'Goha has taken a vow that as long as the old king is alive he will sit at his feet as the crown prince.' Mandlik's heart filled with joy. He whispered to himself: 'Blessed be Goha! Blessed be his love!'

But then he heard someone breathing in the dark. He turned and saw that the fierce hunting dog that had been his brother's companion was sighing as it stood forlorn and quiet in the pitch black. Mandlik's heart seemed to explode. 'My brother!' he cried, and threw himself against the mountain wall. Goha's dagger bounced off the rocks and slashed the Bhil king's chest as the dog's fangs could have. Foxes raised howls of lamentation all across the mountains.

The next morning, a Rajput who was travelling to Veernagar by way of the mountain found the bloodied body of the Bhil king, with Goha's dagger embedded in it. He brought the dagger to Goha and asked: 'King, what have you done? You murdered the Bhil king who gave you shelter and trusted you always?' Immediately, Goha ordered the man's head to be cut off.

He stuck the bloodied knife back in his waistband and wiped his tears with his hands. He consigned Mandlik, whom he had loved more than life itself, and his brother, to the fire of the funeral pyre. Then Goha, the Suryavamshi prince, descended from Suryadev, the Sun God, sat on the throne of the king of the Bhils and began his reign over his dominion.

3

Bappaditya

When the husk of the rice is burnt, it smoulders for a long time and then suddenly turns into a firestorm. Similarly, after Goha passed away, over the years and decades, the anger the Bhils felt towards the Rajputs kept building quietly, little by little. Then, one day, it burst into a blaze that engulfed the forests and the mountains.

For eight generations the Bhils had endured the cruel repression of the Rajput kings in respectful memory of Goha's handsome visage, his boundless kindness and his indomitable courage. If a Rajput king on his way to a hunt spilt the blood of a Bhil passing by with a careless thrust of his spear, the Bhil would recall how Goha had saved an ancestor of his from a fierce tiger and wiped the blood from his chest with his own hands.

When a Rajput prince burnt an entire village just for fun and watched on in glee as it went down, the villagers thought of the time of a great famine when Goha had kept his grand palace and his barns full of grain open to his poor and helpless Bhil subjects for a whole year.

Sometimes when, because of ill luck, a battle was lost, and a cowardly Rajput prince would accuse the Bhil generals of treason and order their heads crushed, one after the other, under the feet of elephants, the soldiers of the Bhil army would wipe their tears and think – alas, once upon a time there was Maharaja Goha, who, when he went to war, took care of them like a brother, protected them like a mother and always fearlessly led his army from the front.

So much tyranny, so much humiliation – yet the innocent hearts of the Bhils remained filled with trust and loyalty to the Rajput kings for eight generations. But then, Bappaditya's father, Nagaditya, began a ghastly reign of terror when he ascended to the throne.

This heartless despot was not satisfied even after burning down the villages of his poor subjects and looting their harvest. He captured thousands of Bhil girls and distributed them among Rajput homes as slaves. It seemed he could not get a good night's sleep without thinking up some new cruelty. But the day Nagaditya passed a law banning the only sport the Bhils knew – the hunting of wild animals – the dam of the Bhils' patience finally broke.

The night before the diktat was issued had been one of pleasant dreams for Nagaditya. The day had dawned cloudy, with a cool breeze blowing and not a hint of dust anywhere. It was a very fine day for a hunt. At once the king got his elephant ready and set off for the jungle. He took only Rajputs that day with him – hordes of them, riding their high stallions. Under the new law, even a little Bhil boy was not permitted to accompany them.

Just as a cheetah in a cage feels agitated and helpless when it spots a prey, so was the state of the Bhils' souls as they sat cooped up in their homes on such a splendid day for a hunt. Nagaditya knew this very well, and that knowledge made his heart dance in delight.

The king rode up to the top of a mountain with his cohorts, their hunting horns creating a great racket. On other days, that thunderous din would make herds of buffaloes rush out of the waters and flee helter-skelter and cause all the birds in the forest to leave their nests and scatter into the sky. Thousands of terrified deer would lose their way and run right to where their killers were waiting for them. Sleeping lions would wake up and tigers would roar. Hunters armed with spears would go after the buffaloes, and others with swords run in search of the lions. But today, however many times Nagaditya blew his horn and however loudly his hunters yelled, no tiger roared, no bird wings fluttered and not a single deer's hoofbeats could be heard. It seemed as if the mountain was in deep slumber.

Nagaditya's eyes turned red with fury. He told his followers: 'Turn your horses around. These wretched Bhils have chased away all the wildlife to some other mountain. So today we will go from village to village, town to town, and hunt herds of Bhils. Those savages are in every way as lowly as animals.'

Waving its trunk and jiggling its ears, the royal elephant began moving towards the fortress of Idarpur. The golden canopy on the elephant's back and the silver-threaded royal chair under it glittered like diamonds. All around it, the two hundred spears held aloft by the Rajput horsemen sparkled in the morning sunlight. 'Speed up!' ordered Nagaditya. And then, suddenly, with a deep roar that seemed to split the mountains, a huge black panther, as if it were a Bhil army commander, appeared at the mouth of the narrow pass before the tyrant, blocking the way of his elephant.

Exhilarated, Nagaditya leant forward on the elephant's back with his lance in his right hand. But the lance stayed in his hand – from the darkness of the forest came a long arrow decorated with giant pitch-black feathers, slicing through the air and shooting straight through his heart. Thus ended this cruel monarch's life at the hands of the Bhils.

Now the Bhils leaped out of the bushes from every side, like thousands of panthers, and painted the mountainside crimson with Rajput blood. Not a single Rajput survived. Only an ebony steed of the king, wearing a caparison of gold, charged through the night-coloured sea of Bhil warriors and galloped away like a gale towards the royal palace.

On the terrace of the Idarpur fortress, the queen was taking a walk in the evening breeze with the child-prince Bappa in her arms. Periodically, she glanced at the mountain where the king had gone for his hunt. Then a hubbub rose from that direction and the queen saw the royal black stallion emerge from the dark forest and come racing down the hilly terrain towards the fortress, pursued by hundreds of Bhils, some brandishing spears, some with bows and arrows.

The queen saw white foam spray from the horse's mouth, like so many pearls, and blood from the centre of its chest sprinkle the ground beneath its feet. Then an arrow flew in like a flaming bolt, parting its black mane and piercing its neck, which was as beautifully arched as a bow, and pinned it to the ground. The king's faithful steed lay writhing in the dust, its head turned towards the fortress. At that moment a spear swooped in over the queen's head and clattered to the floor of the terrace. The queen wrapped the sleeping Bappa with her headscarf and ran downstairs.

The metal clang of weapons and battle cries rose all around as Suryadev sank in the western sky beyond the Malia mountains.

What a terrifying night it was! Countless Bhils had come down from the mountains and forests, and a handful of Rajputs fought them with all their might. Inside the dark palace, Nagaditya's widow sat alone in her bedroom with the five-year-old Bappa clasped to her breast. She called out many times for her maids, but no one answered. She called for the guards to get news of her husband, but they were all busy in battle. Even when they ran through her room they paid no heed to her cries.

Finally, anxious and fearful, the queen covered little Bappa with a small blanket woven from camel hair and, cradling him in her arms, unlocked the massive sandalwood door of her private quarters with a key of gold and peeped out. The night was black, the palace dark. Under great looming stone arches, giant doors with ivory carvings on them stood wide open. The grand palace seemed devoid of all life.

The shocked queen stood at the open doorway, one arm around Bappa at her breast, a bunch of gold keys in her other hand. From the darkness came the sound of footsteps. It was not the *mutch-mutch* of the leather shoes of a Rajput warrior. It was not the *jhini-jhini* tinkle of a maidservant's silver anklets. It was not the *khut-khut* of the wooden clogs that the seventy five-year-old royal head priest wore. This was a stealthy sound, like that of a thief, the *khushh-khaashh* of a snake. It frightened the queen.

Soon, a Bhil chieftain who looked like a demon appeared before her. 'Who are you? What do you want?' asked the queen. The chieftain bellowed like a tiger and said: 'You don't know who I am? I am that miserable Bhil whose daughter your Maharaja gave away to the king of Chittor as a slave. What a happy day this is! With this hand of mine, I shoved my spear into Nagaditya's chest. And with this same hand I'll make a slave of you, drag you away, tied to the end of a rope, along with your son.'

The queen trembled from head to foot. 'Save me, O God!' she cried, and threw the heavy bunch of keys of solid gold at the Bhil chieftain's forehead with all her strength. The fearsome Bhil screamed in pain and dropped to the floor. The queen, clutching little Bappa to her breast, left the palace, half of her heart in howling lament over the death of King Nagaditya, the other half determined to keep her son safe in this time of grave danger.

She kept walking. The stones cut into her feet, the cold froze her hands, she kept losing her way in the dark, but she walked on. How far, how far, how far would she have to go? The path through the mountains seemed to not end anywhere. The queen kept trudging on and the path still seemed to stretch on beyond the horizon. Finally, when dawn broke, she could see a few homes on both sides of the road at the edge of Veernagar. The mountain air was still cold as ice and even the birds had not woken up when Nagaditya's widow, with the prince Bappa in her arms, knocked on the door of the home of Kamalavati in Veernagar.

Eight generations ago, Shiladitya's widow Pushpavati had bequeathed her infant son Goha to Kamalavati. Today, after so many years, Nagaditya's queen entrusted her son, the Gahlot prince Bappa, to the grandson of the grandson of Kamalavati, an aged royal priest, and plunged into her own funeral pyre.

It was early in the morning that the old priest had given shelter to the prince. In the evening, a Bhil girl with two little boys in tow came to his home, also seeking succour. It was their ancestor who had cut his own finger and anointed the Rajput Goha's forehead with the blood-tilak that marks a king. Now, along with the Rajput royal family, they too had been ruined. The rebellious Bhils had burned their home down and thrown them out of the mountains.

The royal priest left Veernagar with the three Bhils and Bappa and lived for some time in the fortress of Bhandir in the kingdom of a Bhil of the Yadu dynasty. But since the king was a Bhil, the priest could not feel fully safe – a day could come when a Bhil might decide to kill the orphan prince. He had promised the queen that he would protect Bappa from all dangers. He decided to leave the Bhil kingdoms for good and came to Nagendranagar with his four wards.

Between the three-peaked Trikoot mountain that rose like three waves of the sea and the Parashar forest, dark as the thickest storm cloud, lay Nagendranagar and nearby was the palace of a Solanki Rajput king. The aged priest made his home on the outskirts of the city. The Bhil girl would take care of all the housework and the prince, with the two brothers Baliya and Dev, would take cows to pasture in the fields and the forest and play with the other shepherd boys.

The priest never revealed to anyone that Bappa was the son of a king. But he wrote down Bappa's lineage on a copper amulet and tied it around the boy's neck. The fear never left him – that some Bhil might one day come to know of Bappa's true identity and kill him.

Bappa grew older. Running around in the fields and meadows, climbing up and down the mountains, his body became tough as iron. When he could hold back with one arm a buffalo that had run wild, when all the other shepherd boys, none of whom knew that he was a prince, began to respect and fear and serve him as their king, the priest felt relieved to a large extent. He then started building Bappa's mind, to match his body.

Every evening, he would sit with Bappa and tell him stories about the Malia mountains, the Bhil rebellion, Rani Pushpavati, Maharaja Shiladitya, the prince Goha and his dear friend Mandlik. As he listened, tears would sometimes well up in Bappa's eyes, sometimes his face would turn red with rage, and sometimes his heart would quake with dread. All night, he would dream of the mantra to Suryadev that Shiladitya's mother had chanted, or the battles with the Bhils in the mountains, and wake up with a start and wonder – when will I too become a king and go to war?

The years went by. One day, when the first full moon in the month of Shravan was sighted, Bappa was wandering in the forest on his own as his pure-white cow grazed on the fresh moist grass. It was the day of Jhulan, when Lord Krishna and his love Radha had ridden a swing hung from the branches of a tree. It was a time of great celebration for Rajputs. Right from the moment the sun rose, groups of shepherd boys, with new clothes on, some with baby brothers and sisters in their arms, some with pots filled with curd on their shoulders, were rushing to the fair at the palace of Nagendranagar's Rajput king to watch the fun and games, and if they were lucky, to earn some quick money. Bappa stayed back alone in the vast forest.

His two dearest friends, Baliya and Dev, holding their sister's hands, asked him many times: 'Brother, will you not come to the palace?' Bappa shook his head. 'No, I will not,' he said. Perhaps he thought: *I have no brother, no sister, no mother. Whose hand can I hold and go with, and to what festival of joy?*

When Baliya and Dev went off gaily with their sister, when the clouds obscured the morning sun, when his cow had grazed its way through field after field and had hidden in some nook behind the trees, when the forest became utterly silent except for the chirping of the cicadas and the soft rustle of leaves, Bappa began to feel lonely and desolate. He took out his little bamboo flute and started playing the tune of a song from the Bhil mountain kingdom that he had heard Baliya and Dev's sister sing.

The words of the song could not be fathomed, yet on this cloudy day this primitive tune mixed with the monsoon wind and wafted all around Bappa like a lullaby half heard in a dream. He seemed to remember that there, towards the west, where the rays of the sun twinkled from the cradle of the clouds, where the thick black clouds massed together to appear as solid as boulders . . . there, under the darkening sky, maybe once upon a time, he had had a home.

He would walk around, holding his mother's hand in the moonlight on the terrace of that home. How beautiful that home was, and how beautiful his mother's smiling face in the moonlight! Fawns roamed on the green grass around that home, parrots flew in to perch on the heads of trees, bunches of flowers bloomed on the mountainside. How bright their colours were, and how sweet the calls of the birds! With teary eyes,

Bappa gazed at the lowering sky and continued to play the Bhil tune on his bamboo flute. The melancholy melody quavered and wept and floated round and round the forest.

In one corner of the forest, the daughter of the Solanki king was playing with her friends to celebrate the full moon of Jhulan. 'Listen, the shepherd-king Krishna himself is playing the flute inside the forest!' said the princess. 'Come, sisters, let us hang a swing from the branches of that champa tree and we will all play Jhulan.'

But they had no ropes to set up a swing with. Here was a forest as dense as the one at Vrindavan, with the same deep rumble of the coming rains, the same sweet sound from afar of the shepherd-king's flute, and a princess as lovely as Radha surrounded by her friends – it was all just as it had been aeons ago, when Krishna and Radha sat on a swing for the first time. How could this day be spoiled for lack of a rope? The princess was despondent.

Once more that flute sounded, like the most melodic birdsong, and music flowed through the forest from one end to the other in a deluge of delight. The princess took off her diamond-studded bracelet, handed it to a friend and said: 'Go, sister, get a rope from that shepherd. Give him this.'

The princess's friend found Bappa, showed him the bracelet and said: 'Can you give the princess some ropes in exchange for this?' Bappa laughed. 'I can,' he said, 'but only if the princess marries me.'

So, in that secluded forest, Bappa the prince put the diamond bracelet on the princess's wrist, hung the swing from the champa tree and sat on it with her, holding her hand. All the princess's friends danced in a circle around the bride and the groom and sang: 'O what joy! O what delight! Krishna on the swing on Jhulan night!'

Then playtime was over because night was setting in. The princess, having married the shepherd, returned to the royal palace. And Bappa sat under the champa tree, its flowers in full bloom, gazing at the giant full moon of Jhulan, thinking – O what joy! O what delight!

Suddenly, a wind from the east blew in, sending the leaves of the trees aflutter and spreading the fragrance of their flowers all around. It then swept off towards the west. As it vanished, two fat raindrops pattered down on the green leaves of the champa tree. Bappa looked up at the sky – a black cloud from the east was advancing steadily towards the west. Thunder boomed in the distance, and lightning flashed. Bappa got to his feet quickly; he remembered that he had to get home.

His milk-white mother cow was still somewhere out in the forest. He untied the ropes from the tree and went in search of the cow.

It was now dark, but countless fireflies sparkled like diamonds in the trees and the soft smell of wet earth pervaded the forest. Bappa went down every path he found, looking for his cow. Then, all of a sudden, behind a dense cane grove, he saw a seer deep in meditation, a rishi who seemed to be lit from within. Right before him, like Mahadev's beloved bull Nandi, stood Bappa's mother cow, absolutely still, her thick milk gushing down like nectar on the head of a marble Shivalinga, the symbol of Lord Shiva's cosmic power. A stunned Bappa stood and watched.

By and by, his meditation over, the great seer's eyes opened, like the petals of a lotus flower at dawn. He laid his head down on the ground before Mahadev, cupped his hands under the cow's udder and drank the flowing milk. Then he turned to Bappa and said: 'Dear son, I am Maharishi Harit. I bless you. May you live long, may you rule the world. I am very pleased with the milk that your mother cow has offered.

'Today, I move on from this world, so what can I give you on my last day on this earth?' he said. 'This is the falchion of the goddess Ma Bhavani, and this is an indestructible set of bow and arrows. This falchion can tear mountains open, and this quiver can conquer the world. Take these. And, dear son, keep this marble idol of the Ekalinga with you; you must pray to Him always without fail. From today, your title is "Regent of Ekalinga"; you shall rule in his name. All the kings who will come after you in your dynasty must sit on the throne with that title.'

Then he strung a fine leather thread over Bappa's shoulder. Having done that, he sat down in a state of samadhi, the deep meditation that would relieve his soul from its body and unite it with the divine. Soon his sacred body burnt down, as if in a blazing fire. Bappa, with the falchion at his waist, the bow and arrows in his hand and the Ekalinga idol on his head, followed the mother cow home. Thunder growled across the skies, like the war drums of the gods.

It was close to dawn now. The festivities were over and the revellers, exhausted and wan-faced, were returning home. Bappa joined them.

But soon Bappa had to leave Nagendranagar. A few days after his wedding, which for both bride and groom had been just an innocent game, an astrologer arrived at the king's court with a marriage proposal for the princess. By evening, news spread all over the kingdom that the astrologer had read the princess's palms and said that she was already married to a foreigner. The king's spies were hunting for that foreigner and the king had ordered that his head be brought to him forthwith.

The news disturbed Bappa, and after a night spent worrying about it, he rose at dawn to prepare to leave the land. Before he left, he revealed all to his foster father, the eighty-five-year-old royal priest: 'Father, bid me farewell. I am now a grown-up man, why should all of you be in peril because of me?'

'Dear son, you do not know who you are,' replied the priest. 'You are a prince whom your mother had bequeathed to me. How can I let you go at this young age, as if you were just some beggar?' Bappa then showed him Ma Bhavani's falchion and the indestructible bow and arrows. 'Father,' he said, 'these will protect me in foreign lands, and I also have Ekalinga-ji.'

The aged priest then raised his arms in joy and blessed Bappa. 'Go, dear son,' he said. 'You are the son of a king, and you have received the weapons of a king. I, an old Brahmin, bless you. May you be the king of the world. If anyone wants to know your identity, read the words on the amulet tied round your neck and reveal to them the hallowed lineage into which you were born and the throne that your ancestors made radiant. Go, dear son, may you be happy.'

After taking leave of the priest, Bappa went to say farewell to the Bhil woman who had taken care of him from as long as he could remember. But this parting was not easy. After much weeping, she said: 'My darling Bappa, if you have to go, then take your brothers Baliya and Dev with you. My heart quakes at the thought of letting you go all alone.' Then she gave the three brothers three burnt rotis.

With Baliya and Dev by his side, Bappa entered deep into the forest of Parashar. The jungle appeared to be endless. Here the trunks of great trees pushed up towards the sky, like giant columns of stone, and the flying peacocks made the woods glow. Somewhere further ahead, a massive python lay still after having swallowed a goat. There were places where one could hear tigers roar, and elsewhere where you heard only sweet birdsong. In some clearings, the sun shone golden on the green grass but in the nooks the dark was as deep and blue as kohl. Bappa kept walking on with his two brothers, fearless of heart, Ma Bhavani's falchion in hand.

It took them three days and three nights to cross the vast forest of Parashar. Prince Bappa and the brothers ate nothing but the three burnt rotis. After they cleared the forest, they traversed through village after village, through kingdom after kingdom, enduring many a monsoon and winter along the way. Bappa finally reached the city of Chittor, capital of Mewar, ruled by Raja Maan of the Maurya dynasty.

Great preparations were being made in the kingdom for war against the Muslim invaders. Heavy weaponry, provisions and tents were being loaded on the backs of elephants and camels; more arms and provisions on bullock carts; and drinking water and ghee, to be used for cooking, were being poured into huge drums.

Rajput soldiers with colourful turbans on their heads and carrying spears kept guard on every street. All over the city the king's spies were on the lookout for agents of the invaders. Raja Maan, his chieftains in tow, was himself riding around on his horse, inspecting all the arrangements.

Bappa had never seen such a tumult, such crowds, such a big city, so many large houses made of stone. Nagendranagar had houses, but they had earthen walls, and its temples now seemed very small. Bappa stood by the side of the main road, amazed, and Baliya and Dev gaped at the enormous elephants as they lumbered by. At that point Raja Maan came down on his horse, accompanied by his chieftains. The golden caparison of his white stallion trailed on the ground; a splendid umbrella hung over the king's head, shading him from the sun; and he was being cooled by two men who flanked him, waving huge fans made of peacock feathers.

This was the right time to meet the king, decided Bappa. Dragging Baliya and Dev along by their arms, he ran right to the middle of the road, held Ma Bhavani's falchion to his forehead and touched his head to the ground to show his respect for the king. 'Who are you? What do you want?' asked Raja Maan.

'I am the son of a Rajput king,' replied Bappa. 'I wish to live as a king under your shelter.'

A beggar was claiming to be the son of a king! All the chieftains smirked. But Raja Maan looked at Bappa's massive physique, his handsome face, his indestructible bow and arrows and Ma Bhavani's falchion, and immediately he thought – this was a man with an extraordinary destiny, and God had been kind enough to send him this great warrior to aid him in this war against the invaders. He took his silver-threaded shawl off, draped it over Bappa's shoulders and ordered a black steed to be brought for him.

'Maharaj, please get horses for my Bhil brothers too,' said Bappa. Then, after Baliya and Dev were astride their horses, he mounted his black stallion. At once he seemed to rise above the heads of all the generals and soldiers, like a mountain emerging from an ocean, far taller than any man around. The people watching from the roadside began saying: 'Yes, he is surely a great warrior. Look at his face, look at his powerful body.'

Everyone started to cheer, but the king's generals, seeing this beggar in the royal shawl towering over them, resented Raja Maan for what he had done. And as over the days the king appeared to get fonder of Bappa and began treating him as his blue-eyed boy, the commanders burned with ever-growing jealousy.

The day of the war with the invaders arrived. On that morning, all the chieftains from all the lands and all the aged generals stood in Raja Maan's court before him and said in unison: 'Maharaj, we have staked our lives for you so many times in so many wars, only because you loved us. Today, Maharaj, if you have forgotten that love and placed this streetside mendicant above all of us, if Bappa is now dearer to you than life itself, if he is more trustworthy than all of us, then what is the use of us? Make Bappa the supreme commander for the war. Our valour has been seen on many an occasion, now let us see how this new commander fights the war.'

Raja Maan was thunderstruck at this cruel statement from the chieftains, whom he had always thought of as eternally loyal to him. He sat in silence, unable to utter a word. Then, in that magnificent court, the brave fifteen-year-old Bappaditya, surrounded on all sides by the rebellious noblemen, stood up and said: 'Please hear this, Maharaj! All the most powerful chieftains of Rajasthan are saying that in this time of great danger Bappa should be the commander and fight the war. Let it be so then.'

Raja Maan looked all around helplessly. Then he said softly: 'Let it be so.' As he went inside the palace through one door of the court, close to fainting and leaning on his servants, Bappaditya went out through another to marshal his army.

The chieftains hung their heads in shame. They had thought that the fifteen-year-old Bappa would never dare to go to war, that he would be humiliated in front of the full court. When this courageous boy asked the king, fearlessly and with a smile on his face, to give him charge of the coming terrible war, their astonishment knew no bounds.

And then they were even more astounded when Bappa, whom they had detested as a tramp from the streets – that fifteen-year-old boy – won the war and returned to Chittor, the Rajput capital regarded as the crown jewel of all of Rajasthan. He entered Chittor on an auspicious day at an auspicious hour, and hundreds of thousands of Rajput citizens showered their blessings on him and wildly cheered him. What a day it was for Rajasthan – a day of so much joy, bringing them so much confidence!

Bappa became the chief of the Mewar army. The day he returned to Chittor after making sure that Rajasthan was safe from the invaders, all the old and sorely disappointed chieftains left Raja Maan's court. The king tried his utmost to keep them back. He pleaded with them to stay back, and in the end even sent the religious guru of the royal family to speak to them, but all of it was of no avail. The chieftains sent their final decision to the king through an emissary: 'We have eaten your salt and we are grateful to you. For one year we shall show you no enmity. But when the year ends, we shall meet on the battlefield.'

That one year was a time of many a terrible conspiracy and much deadly and secret conniving. At the end of the year, fooled by the chieftains into believing that Raja Maan would betray him, Bappa joined them as their general and set off to wage war against the king.

Raja Maan was grief-stricken when he heard that Bappa was coming to seize his throne – Bappa, whom he had picked up from the dust of the street and raised to the royal court, whose tattered attire he had covered with his own silver shawl, a boy he had loved more than life itself. Now this orphan had forgotten all that and was coming to capture his kingdom! Tears streaked down his cheeks.

The elderly king went to war alone with a platoon of loyal soldiers. That was his last battle; Raja Maan lost his life on the battlefield at Bappa's hands.

Sixteen-year-old Bappa married the princess of Devbandar and ascended the throne of Chittor, assuming many titles – Hindu Crown, Hindu Sun and King of All Kings. The two Bhil brothers, Baliya and Dev, anointed him with the royal tilak of blood on his forehead and received two villages as gifts. That day, Bappa made it a rule that all the future kings of his dynasty would have to get their coronation tilak from the descendants of these two Bhils before they could sit on the throne. That edict is followed to this day.

When Bappaditya announced this new law in Rajasthan, most people thought it was just a whim of the new king. But the scholars in the late Raja Maan's court wondered: Does this mean that he is a Gahlot prince from Goha's lineage? After all, it was only the Suryavamshis – men of the Sun Dynasty – who followed the practice of getting the coronation tilak from a Bhil! Could it be, then, that Maharaja Bappa was the son of Nagaditya, whose queen had been the princess of Chittor, Raja Maan's sister? That would make Raja Maan Bappa's maternal uncle!

What could be more shameful than this? Bappa had committed a monstrous sin – capturing his uncle's throne through subterfuge. He was no better than a common thief! It would be a grave sin to even live in this venal man's kingdom! The scholars never came to Bappa's court again. One by one, they all left Chittor to settle in other lands.

Alas! If only the wise men had known that Bappa was innocent! He had never even dreamt that Raja Maan could be his uncle. He had heard stories from his foster father, the royal priest, about the rebellion of the Bhils, of Raja Goha, Gayab and Gayabi. But he did not know that Raja Nagaditya, whose brutal tyranny had caused the honest Bhils to rise up against the Rajputs, was his father. He did not know that Goha, the infant prince whom the queen Pushpavati had bequeathed to Kamalavati before plunging into her own funeral pyre, was his ancestor. Bappa had always thought that he was the prince of some minor state.

When he had come back to Chittor after marrying the princess of Devbandar, he had brought with him a golden idol of Banmata Devi. He had installed the idol in a marble temple inside the royal palace. He would do puja to the idol twice every day, at dawn and at dusk.

Many years passed, and Bappa was nearing old age when, one day, as he rose after having prostrated himself before Banmata Devi, the thread that tied the copper amulet around his neck broke. All these years the amulet had remained just as it was. In fact, because it had been there for so long, Bappa was not even aware any more that he had something around his neck. Today, when it fell out from under his twenty-strand necklace of diamonds and pearls, Bappa was startled. 'Oh, I had forgotten about this!' he thought. 'Inside it is my history – who I am and where I came from! Today I will get to know everything!'

Happily, he gave the amulet to his queen and said: 'Please read this out to me.' Bappa was illiterate. The queen sat at his feet and began reading out what was written on the amulet.

On one side of the amulet was written: 'Home address: Trikoot mountain, Nagendranagar, Parashar forest.'

Bappa put his hand on his queen's shoulder with a smile on his face. 'That was where I spent my childhood,' he said. 'Oh, all the games I played and all the fun I had! The Trikoot mountain, the sombre face of the eighty-year-old priest, that moonlit night of Jhulan at Nagendranagar, the sweet smile of the Solanki princess, I can still remember all of it, as if it were a dream I had.

'I have asked so many people so many times, but there are so many three-peaked mountains in this world, how would I ever be able to find the one I was looking for?' he continued. 'If I could have only told them that the cloud-coloured mountain that rose like three swells of the sea was called Trikoot, if I could have told them that that small city was called Nagendranagar, if I had known that the dense forest where I played with the other shepherd boys, where on the day of Jhulan I married the Solanki princess, was called Parashar, there would not have been any of this confusion at all! This is the result of not learning to read and write. After all these years, will I ever be able to get the aged priest and the Solanki princess back? Please read out what else is written there.'

The queen turned the amulet and read: 'Birthplace: Malia mountain. Father: Nagaditya. Mother: Princess of Chittor. Name: Bappa.'

The queen's wide eyes widened even more in amazement. She sat frozen at Bappa's feet, on the carpet that was as soft and beautiful as a bed of flowers, holding the amulet in her hand. And on his bed built of ivory, Bappa stared at a ring on a finger of his right hand with a gem as big and red as a drop of blood and kept thinking: *What have I done! Instead of disciplining the Bhils who killed my father, I killed my uncle, with this very hand, and am sitting on his throne!*

'Queen, I am a horrible sinner,' he said. 'I am not fit to sit on the throne of Chittor. My mission for the rest of my life will be to avenge the murder of my father and atone for killing a blood relative.'

That very day, Bappaditya, Regent of Ekalinga, said farewell to everyone and set off from Chittor with a force of ten thousand elite soldiers who owed allegiance only to the Ekalinga. He directed all his rage at the Bhil kingdom in the Malia mountains. He conquered Malia, razed the Bhil kingdom to the ground and moved on.

He kept moving, conquering kingdom after kingdom – Kashmir, Kabul, Isfahan, Kandahar, Iran and Touran. All his desires were fulfilled. The conquest of the Malia mountains satisfied half of his yearnings – that of avenging the murder of his father. And bringing half the world under the rule of Chittor assuaged much of the guilt he felt over killing his uncle. But where was the peace of mind and rest for the soul that he so desperately sought?

After a full day's battle and the conquest of a new

kingdom, as he sat exhausted in his tent, he would look out on the barren battlefield awash with light under the full moon and remember the radiant face of the Solanki princess on the swing hung from the champa tree on that night of Jhulan.

Even when he moved from his tent to the palace of a defeated king and drifted off to sleep in a bed of gold, listening to the sweet melodies played by musicians seated on the roof of the palace gateway, the song that the princess's friends had sung that night as they danced round and round the swing hung on the champa tree would float through his dreams and eat into his soul.

Finally, when he arrived at Nagendranagar and saw that the earthen walls of the little thatch-roofed cottage where he had grown up had turned to dust, when he saw that the Solanki royal palace was now an empty, silent, dark shell, with no princess or any of her friends, Bappaditya's heart shattered. Like a madman who had lost all hope of peace and quiet, he roamed from land to land with his all-conquering army, desperately seeking some serenity.

Meanwhile, the vast royal palace of Chittor lay desolate, its throne abandoned, with only a lonely queen living in one of its dark corners.

One day, wandering from kingdom to kingdom,

Bappa reached Gayaninagar in Ballavipur, where the siblings Gayab and Gayabi had seen their first light.

As the sixteen-year-old general of Raja Maan, Bappa had chased the entire army of Sultan Salim out of Gayaninagar and returned to Chittor. Today, so many years later, when his black hair had turned grey and dark circles had grown under his eyes, when his iron body had grown soft, when the world seemed aged and jaded in his mind, he had come again to Gayaninagar. And he remembered the story of Gayab and Gayabi.

Bappaditya did his puja of the Sun God at the sacred lake of Suryakund and went to rest in the marble bedroom of Gayaninagar's royal palace. In the dead of night he was suddenly woken up by a sweet melody. He came out to the flagstone terrace. Before him, the city's massive mosque stood bathed white in the moonlight. There was not a soul to be seen anywhere. Bappaditya stood under the sky and listened to the song.

He had heard this song somewhere! And then a gust of wind from the south brought the words more clearly to his ears. Bappaditya was shaken to his core. 'O what joy! O what delight! Krishna on the swing on Jhulan night!' This was the song, the Jhulan song of Nagendranagar's Rajput princess!

Bappaditya leaned out over the parapet and looked

down. A beggar woman stood on the street below, singing. At once he asked for the woman to be brought up to him. Soon the mendicant was standing before Bappaditya the emperor on the moonlit terrace. 'Who are you?' he asked. 'Are you the Solanki princess of Nagendranagar? Did you ever marry a shepherd boy on the night of Jhulan?'

The woman looked at Bappa's face for a long time, then smiled a little and said: 'Maharaj, what is this joke that you play on a poor beggar in the middle of the night?'

'So you are not the princess?' asked Bappaditya.

The woman sighed and replied: 'Yes, I used to be a princess once but am just a beggar now. Maharaj, I am the daughter of Sultan Salim. The day you seized our kingdom, when you were only sixteen, I had stood on this very terrace in this very palace and watched you. How handsome you were, how powerful your body looked! But what do I see today? That body is no more, that smile is gone! Who did this to you? Who is this Rajput princess you are so obsessed with that you are running around like a lunatic all over the world?'

'Let that be,' said Bappaditya. 'Sing me that song once more.' The mendicant began singing: 'O what joy! O what delight! Krishna on the swing on Jhulan night!' The emperor, all his sorrows forgotten, stood enraptured and could only gaze at her face.

The song ended. 'Princess, what should I give you?' Bappaditya asked.

Said the mendicant: 'If I still had a kingdom, I would have asked you to marry me and make me your begum, but I do not harbour any such hopes any more. I am but a beggar now. Make me your slave and keep me close to you.'

'You are not meant to be a slave,' replied Bappaditya. 'I will make you my begum. I want you to stay with me forever and sit by me and sing that song.'

The next day, Bappaditya married the Muslim princess and went off with her to Khorasan. But no one knows whether – resting in the beautiful private rose garden of his palace by a fountain that threw fragrant rose water into the air, and sipping the finest of wines and listening to his begum sing ghazals from Persia, and the Jhulan song from Hindustan . . . no one knows whether he found the peace that he had been looking so hard for.

Bappaditya passed away when he was one hundred years old. In the east lived his Hindu queen and Hindu subjects, on the west, in Iranistan, his Muslim begum and the Pathan tribes. The Hindus wanted to put his body on the pyre, and the Nowshera Pathans began arranging a Muslim burial. In the end, when the giant velvet shroud that had hymns to Suryadev calligraphed on one side and to Allah on the other was lifted from his body, there was nothing there – only masses of lotus flowers and roses.

The queen of Chittor took the lotus flowers and floated them on the waters of the sacred lake in the temple of Banmati Devi. The Irani begum took a single rose and placed it at the centre of Bappaditya's beloved garden, next to the rose-water fountain.

And that day, exactly halfway between Hindustan and Iranistan, on a peak of the Hindu Kush mountains, a sanyasin placed the body of an emperor wrapped in diamonds and dazzling jewels on a pyre and cried: 'My sisters, please sing that song.' Four sanyasins moved round and round the pyre and sang: 'O what joy! O what delight!'

The sanyasin was the Solanki princess and the body was Bappaditya's. The two had spent their lives looking for each other but could never be together in this mortal world.

4

Padmini

The first Muslim invaders came to Bharat during the time of Bappaditya. Many kings of the Sun Dynasty – the Suryavamsha – have sat on the throne of Chittor after him. But the story of the dynasty is a bloody one: of brother fighting brother, of terrible battles, of a sea of blood and tears shed over the throne. The tales of only a few noble and valiant kings remain etched in Rajput hearts today.

One of them is Raja Khoman, who saved Chittor from the invaders twenty-four times and even kept Al Mamoun, a son of Haroun Al Rashid, the famous Caliph of Baghdad, about whom we read in *The Arabian Nights*, prisoner in his Chittor palace for a long time. Even today, when blessing someone, many Rajputs say: 'May Khoman protect you.'

Another is Maharaja Samarsingh, a great warrior and as devout a follower of the principles of Dharma as Khoman. When Samarsingh sat on the throne with his hair tied in a bun like a Naga sanyasi, wearing a garland of lotus seeds and holding Ma Bhavani's falchion in his hand, it seemed like the Regent of Ekalinga had truly come down from the heights of the Kailash mountain to rule over the earth.

When Shahabuddin Ghori – whom the British called Muhammad Ghori – came to seize the throne of Dilli, half of Bharat, including Samarsingh, with thirteen thousand Rajputs and his son Kalyan, went to fight the invaders alongside Raja Prithviraj Chauhan on the banks of the river Kagar. That would be Samarsingh's last battle. Prithviraj was Samarsingh's closest friend, the younger brother of his beloved wife Pritha. The two men loved each other. Perhaps that is why, in the battle of Kagar, Samarsingh paid off a life's worth of debt to his friend and left forever.

On the day of the battle, amidst storms and rains so terrifying that it seemed like the world was about to come to an end, Prithviraj's massive army, with all its hundreds of thousands of soldiers and all their horses and elephants, was thrown into total disarray. When there was no hope of victory, when almost all the kings who were supposed to be fighting for Prithviraj had fled back to their kingdoms, fearing for their lives, it was Samarsingh alone who chose the cause above his wife, family, crown and throne, and fought by his friend's side, losing his life in the fierce battle with the invaders.

The sandy banks of the Kagar river turned red with the blood of this saint, his sixteen-year-old son Kalyan and thirteen thousand Rajputs. Prithiviraj was taken prisoner and the throne of Dilli was captured by Badshah Shahabuddin.

So many centuries later, no one remembers those kings who had sworn their loyalty to Prithviraj and then run away. But the tale of the devout and valiant warrior Samarsingh, who cared little for his own life when fighting for his dearest friend, has been immortalized by the beautiful songs composed by Rajput poets. Even today travelling minstrels roam the streets of Rajputana singing these ballads.

A hundred years after Samarsingh's death. Rana Lakshmansingh sat on the throne of Chittor, and Pathan Badshah Alauddin on the throne of Dilli. One day, Lakshmansingh's uncle Bhimsingh returned to Chittor from across the sea with his new bride, Padmini, princess of the island kingdom of Sinhala. Just as the fragrance of the padma – the lotus – spreads joy across the entire lake where it blooms and then wafts beyond the horizons, stories of the beauty and talent of Rani Padmini, lovely as Goddess Lakshmi herself, who resides in a lotus flower, entranced all of Bharat. From the little cottages of the poorest of all to the grandest palaces of emperors, there was no woman in the land who was so beautiful and so talented in every way as she.

Bhimsingh was spending his days with his wondrously beauteous wife in the cool private chambers of his marble palace at the centre of a lake on the edge of Chittor. At around the same time, one evening the Pathan Badshah Alauddin was enjoying the pleasant spring breeze as he reclined on his ivory divan on the terrace of his bedroom in Dilli. The moon shone bright and his Piyari Begum was sitting next to him, a glass of sherbet in her hand. At her feet, one of the Begum's new maids was playing the sarangi and singing a ghazal.

Suddenly the Badshah exclaimed: 'I am tired of these ghazals from Arabia! Sing me a song from Hindustan!' So Piyari Begum's maid began playing a new tune on her sarangi and sang:

A flower blooms in Hindustan that is beyond all compare
What is that flower, what can that flower be?

It is the padma, the lotus, which blooms out of the
azure water all around.
The gods gaze at the flower, men gape at the flower,
the roaring waves of the endless ocean surround and
guard the flower.
No one dares to cross the ocean, no one dares to pluck
the flower in the king's garden.
For even the gods tremble in fear when they think of
this king.

Alauddin was furious. 'I am the Badshah of Hindustan,' he shouted. 'Neither do I care for any king, nor am I afraid of any gods. Piyari! I will leave tomorrow and go pluck this flower.'

The maid continued with her singing:

Who was the fortunate man who crossed the ocean?
Who was the valiant who picked the flower?
From the line of the great warriors of Mewar – Rana
Bhimsingh – the handsome and fearless one.

Alauddin sat up straight on his velvet rug. The song ended on a note of joy:

The flower lives deep inside the citadel of Chittor
The one whom the poets of Bharat sing of, is she not beyond all compare?
Who on this earth can ever match her?
Hail Rana Bhimsingh, hail the queen Rani Padmini who lights up Chittor's royal garden.

For quite some time the words 'Rani Padmini who lights up Chittor's royal garden' kept echoing in Alauddin's head. Staring up at the sky, he asked: 'Maid, have you seen Padmini with your own eyes? Is she truly that beautiful?'

'O King of the World,' replied the girl. 'Before I came to Dilli, I used to earn my living in Chittor, singing and dancing. On the night of Padmini's wedding, I danced in the queen's mahal – her private palace.'

Alauddin rested his chin on his palm and went into deep thought. After some time he said: 'Piyari, I wish to bring Padmini here.'

'O Shahenshah, King of Kings,' said Piyari Begum, 'if I could have my way, I would pull the moon off the sky and keep it in a small gold box for you to savour.'

Alauddin did not like this reply. He was the Badshah of Dilli who held half of Bharat in his fist, and he would not be able to capture a mere Rajput queen? Sombre-faced, he got up and left, thinking: *Let it be, Piyari. When I get Padmini, you will have to live as her slave.*'

The very next day, Alauddin left for Chittor with hundreds of thousands of soldiers. And wherever the Pathan army went, it burnt and plundered all the farmland and villages and towns on both sides along its path.

While Alauddin advanced, all of Chittor was caught up in a wave of springtime joy. Holi was around the corner – 'Holi hai! It is Holi!' Every house was a riot of colour; the sound of laughter was everywhere and the bright yellow that symbolizes the season blossomed in every nook and cranny. It was in the midst of all this celebration that the news arrived that Alauddin was on his way to Chittor with his huge army. All the joy, all the happiness in Chittor, was instantly extinguished, like a lamp in the face of a gale. The beautiful songs in the Dhrupad tradition describing spring sung in the royal court came to a halt. The sweet melodies to which 'Come let's celebrate the month of Phagun!' were playing in the palaces where the queens lived were silenced. The musicians who had been playing Raga Basant – the raga of the season – from the tops of the gates of the temple of Gopal-ji fell silent.

Every home in Chittor, still coloured red with gulaal

powder and the roses with which people had been preparing to play Holi, now resounded with the clang of weapons as planning began for another sport – a deadly one that is played on open battlefields with the blood of the players and the slashes of their sabres. The black pennants of the Pathan king soon appeared, like a swarm of vultures, on the Mewar desert. 'Shut the gates,' ordered Bhimsingh. At once the seven great gates of Chittor closed with a boom that echoed all around.

Alauddin had expected that he would be able to just walk in and capture Padmini. But now he saw that row upon row of Rajputs encircled and guarded Padmini day and night, much like the ribs that protect the heart from all sides. Penetrating the seven gates of the palace and capturing Padmini from the core of the fort was impossible. Crossing the oceans, which the maid's song had mentioned, seemed easy in comparison. The Badshah ordered camp to be set up at the foot of the mountain.

Late that night, after finishing the arrangements for war, Bhimsingh came to Padmini and said: 'Padmini, do you want to see the ocean? An ocean like the endless blue one on the shore of which stood your palace in Sinhala?'

'Please don't joke!' said Padmini. 'How will an ocean appear in the middle of this land of deserts?' Bhimsingh took Padmini's hand and the two climbed up to the terrace of the fort. The sky was a moonless, starless black. Then Padmini saw, under that black sky, an expanse even blacker, that stretched from the gates of the fort and across the desert to beyond the horizon. She said: 'Rana, I never knew that there was an ocean here. Look at the little white waves!'

Bhimsingh laughed. 'Padmini, this is not that sort of ocean,' he said. 'That is the Pathan Badshah's army arrayed in square formation. Those are the camps that look like a cascade of waves, and the rising and falling rumble of the sea that you hear is the hubbub of the soldiers. I think that the blue ocean from whose heart I had plucked you like a golden lotus and brought you here has come, in the garb of this giant square, to take you away from me. I wonder how we can cross this extremely dangerous ocean.'

Bhimsingh was about to say something more when a black owl came swooping down over their heads with a shrill screech. The cold wind from its wings blew over their faces on that dark roof like a pair of chilly hands touching their cheeks. Padmini, startled, clasped the Rana's hand and they made their way down. But she could not sleep at all that night. She kept thinking: *What an ill omen! What an ill omen!*

The next day, as the first light of dawn appeared in the eastern sky, a Rajput horseman reached the Pathan camp. Badshah Alauddin was at that time seated in his silver chair, deep in his morning religious ritual of reciting the holy texts. The news was conveyed to him: An emissary of Rana Lakshmansingh had arrived. 'Bring him to me,' ordered the Badshah.

The Rana's messenger bowed to the Badshah three times, then held himself erect and said: 'The Rana wishes to know what the dispute is between him and the Badshah that the Badshah has come to Chittor with such a large army.'

'I have no enmity with the Rana,' replied Alauddin. 'I consider myself an uncle of the Rana. I have come to beg Bhimsingh for Padmini. I shall return to my land as soon as I receive her.'

'O King of Kings,' said the emissary. 'You don't know the Rajput race. Forget the Rana, even poor and lowly Rajputs like me will give up our lives but not our honour. Please relinquish all hope of getting the queen. Instead, if the King of Kings desires something else . . .'

Alauddin interrupted the emissary midway and said: 'The Badshah of Hindustan has only one thing to say

– Padmini or war.' The Rana's representative stepped back, bowed three times again and left.

That evening, all the Rajput chieftains gathered in Chittor's royal court to discuss how the kingdom could be saved from the aggressors. Chittor was the crown jewel of Rajasthan. It was dearer to the Rajputs than their lives. Muslim invaders had captured much of Bharat; many great Hindu kingdoms had not only been plundered but had even disappeared from the face of the earth. But the throne of Chittor had remained as it had been since the days of yore – resolute and independent. How could Chittor be saved today from the greatest threat it had ever faced?

The debate continued for hours and many views were presented. Finally, Rana Bhimsingh stood up. 'If Chittor faces such ruin because of Padmini,' he said, 'let us hand Padmini over to the Pathans. I will have no regrets about this. Who comes first – Chittor or Padmini?' He then looked in the direction of the marble-latticed partition at one end of the court hall, behind which the queens of Chittor sat watching the proceedings, and then towards the throne. 'Maharana,' he said. 'What do you say?'

'If all the chieftains agree,' said Lakshmansingh, 'then that should be our decision and duty.' And then the biggest leader of all the chieftains loyal to the throne rose. 'A threat to the Ranas is a threat to all of us,' he said. 'An insult to the Ranas is an insult to us. Rani Padmini is not only Rana Bhimsingh's wife, she is also our queen. How can we send her off to be the begum of a Pathan? The world over, people will ask: "Was there not a single man in Rajasthan willing to fight for their Rana and their queen?" Maharana, we are ready. Give us your command and we will go to war.'

'There is no need right now for war,' said the Maharana. 'Keep the gates closed. Alauddin can sit as long as he likes with his army surrounding Chittor.' The entire court burst into cheers. Every chieftain and warlord of Chittor stood up, unsheathed his sword and raised it high above his head. In one voice the court shouted: 'Hail the Maharana! Hail Bhimsingh! Hail Rani Padmini!'

The court was dismissed. A red handkerchief with a lotus embroidered on it in gold thread floated down from behind the marble lattice at one end of the court hall among the faithful warlords. They tied the blood-red cloth to the head of a spear and left the court, shouting; 'Hail the queen!'

Days passed. Alauddin waited in his camp with his hundreds of thousands of troops surrounding and laying siege to Chittor. The Badshah had been hoping that the Rajputs, locked up inside the fort, would run out of food and seek peace to save their lives and hand Padmini over. But months went by, and then a full year, but there was no sign of any proposal for a peace treaty. The monsoon came and went, and then winter, and then it was summer once more.

Alauddin's soldiers were now getting restless and pining to return to Dilli. What fun it was during summer at Chandni Chowk in Dilli! People were living it up in the taverns there while here they were, come hail or frost, stuck in an open field in this foreign land. One could not even get nice paan or tobacco, nor was there any garden to stroll in. There was no sweet tune to be heard anywhere that could make them forget their troubles. The people here were rough and lacked taste; their songs were bereft of melody, just as their paans were coarse and their tobacco harsh. There was no way one could be content in this land of barbarians.

Alauddin noticed that his troops, hanging around idly, were getting increasingly restive. He wanted to continue his siege of Chittor for some more time, but for this it was essential that the soldiers remained calm and motivated. The Badshah then started to take his soldiers out hunting in groups.

Things changed one evening, when he was returning to camp after a hunt. On one side the green fields of maize were turning a deep indigo in the spreading dark; and on the other was the citadel of Chittor, perched like a bank of clouds on the mountaintop. In between lay a narrow winding path, along which went first the Pathan hunters, carrying the deer they had killed on their shoulders and singing gaily, then the noblemen, some on horses and some on elephants, and bringing up the rear, Badshah Alauddin, one hand holding the reins of his horse, and a huge falcon tied with a chain of gold to the wrist of the other.

As he rode, he mused: So many months had gone by, yet he had been unable to conquer Chittor. The soldiers were eager to go back to Dilli. How much longer could he keep them distracted? Padmini, for whom he had made this arduous journey with such a vast army to this foreign land . . . he had not even managed to set his eyes on her. The Badshah looked at the giant falcon on his wrist. 'I wish I had two wings so I could swoop down on Chittor like this deadly bird and snatch Padmini right from the heart of the fort,' he muttered to himself.

Suddenly, in the gathering twilight, the falcon heard the sound of flapping wings somewhere and shook its own, puffed up its shoulders and sat up erect on the

Badshah's wrist. Alauddin understood that his hunter bird had sensed prey. He looked up at the sky and saw a pair of green lover birds flying overhead, like two pieces of emerald. The Badshah stopped his horse and freed the falcon from its golden chain. It rose swiftly and silently from its master's wrist into the darkening sky, spread its wings and hovered perfectly still for a moment far above the heads of the hunters. It then dropped down like a stone from a height of three hundred yards right between the two birds.

One of the birds began to scream in terror. It flew around, confused, while the other, caught in the falcon's talons, could only wriggle helplessly. Alauddin whistled to the falcon to come down. The trained hunter let go of its prey and came back to its master's wrist, and the little green bird, half dead from fear, fell to the ground. The delighted Badshah ordered it to be picked up and galloped towards his camp.

The mate of the captured bird, crying in distress, followed the hunters from the air for a long time through the dusk that was now turning black. Finally, slowly, it came down to the small cage held by a nobleman, inside which its broken-winged companion struggled and wept, and sat down fearlessly on the roof of the cage. The nobleman was astonished. 'What amazing courage!'

he exclaimed. 'Seeing its husband in danger, the wife has come and surrendered to us on its own!'

Alauddin was riding along, lost in thought. But hearing the nobleman's words, an idea struck him – *If I can capture Bhimsingh, then Rani Padmini may give herself up to me.*

After returning to the camp, the Badshah stayed up all night, trying to think up plots to capture Bhimsingh and imprison him. He began negotiations with Chittor. In a day or two the two sides agreed that Alauddin would go back to Dilli peacefully with his entire Pathan army. All that he wanted in return was to be allowed a glimpse of Padmini's face in a mirror, and that for as long as he was alone inside Chittor fort, the Maharana would be responsible if any harm came to him.

The Badshah began to get ready to visit Chittor. He had not imagined in his wildest dreams that his quarry would walk into his trap so soon. With great joy, he conferred with his Pathan noblemen and thrashed out the details of his plan. Early one evening, he bathed in rose water, put on a set of velvet clothes, a pearl necklace and a turban studded with diamonds and emeralds, and mounted a white horse. His stirrups were forged from gold. About two hundred Pathan warriors accompanied him. They did not fear for their lives – after all, war was the only trade they knew.

The Badshah rode alone up the mountain to the fort, and the Pathan horsemen first went back to their camp from the foot of the mountain and then, one by one, stealthily worked their way back close to the fort under cover of the fading light of dusk and hid in a mango orchard on the side of the road.

As Suryadev sank behind a colossal cloud on Chittor's western sky, Badshah Alauddin, arm in arm with Rana Bhimsingh, arrived at the grand marble hall of Padmini's palace. There was no one else present in the great expanse of the hall, but the light from thousands of candles seemed to create a splendid new day as they reflected off the white stones.

The Rana sat the Badshah down on a golden seat of honour and presented him a cup of sherbet. 'Please have some of this sherbet, Shahenshah,' he said.

Alauddin, cup in hand, began to get worried. *If this drink has poison in it, this venture will be a complete disaster*, he thought. He had heard somewhere that Rajput women, when fearing humiliation from enemies, often served them lethal drinks.

The Badshah hesitated. Rana Bhimsingh understood what was on his mind and smiled. 'O King of Kings, do not be afraid that there might be poison in this drink,' he said. 'When the Maharana himself has promised that he should be held responsible if any harm comes to you, be assured that you can take a tour of all of Chittor on your own and not a single Rajput will dare to lay a hand on you. We look upon guests as gods.'

'No, no, I am not worried about that,' the Badshah replied in some haste. 'In fact, what I was thinking was this – can you not trust me without any fear, the way I have trusted you today?'

But even as he spoke these words, Alauddin's heart trembled at the thought of taking a sip of the sherbet. But he drank it all up slowly and then sat in silence for a long time. At last, when he realized that instead of suffering the horrible effects of a poison, his body and mind actually felt more fresh, he turned to Bhimsingh and said: 'Why delay any further? If I can just have a glimpse of the amazingly beautiful Rani Padmini, I will be a happy man and bid you goodbye.'

Rana Bhim then pulled the curtain back from over an enormous mirror that had come from the land of Aleppo. In that mirror, as perfectly clear as a pool of the purest water, appeared the radiance of Padmini's beauty, making everything around glow like the light from many thousands of lamps.

The Badshah looked and looked at the image in the mirror – the pitch-black eyes, the graceful eyebrows, the hands as soft as lotus petals, the two lovely scarlet feet with their curved anklets, the long wheat-coloured dress with pearls woven into it in flowery patterns, the pink head scarf with its gold borders, the emerald bracelets, the sapphire-bejewelled fingers, the sparkling diamond nose ring. The Badshah was spellbound – was this a human being or an angel?

He could not sit still any more. He got up from his seat and rushed towards the gigantic mirror with arms outstretched, to grasp the shadow Padmini who stood inside, like the demon Rahu who desires to swallow the moon and bring about an eclipse. Bhimsingh called out: 'Shahenshah, do not touch Padmini!'

The Rana suddenly felt as if his innocent and virtuous queen was actually standing at one end of the hall and trembling with fear at the insults and dishonours that this man could subject her to. Furious, he strode down the hall, picked up a heavy gold cup and threw it with all his might at the mirror, striking it right at its centre. The sound of the huge mirror shattering into a hundred pieces echoed all around.

Startled, Alauddin jumped three steps back. He realized that he had been extremely ill-mannered to have run towards the queen like a madman and that he should ask the Rana's forgiveness for this.

Turning towards the Rana, the Badshah said: 'Rana, what I did was completely wrong. If someone had come to my palace and behaved in such a manner, I would have ordered that his head be cut off. Please forgive me.' After much pleading and wheedling, he managed to pacify the Rana.

It was late in the night that he got up to take leave of Bhimsingh. The Rana had by now drunk many cups of the tasty sherbet, which had cheered him up, and a person no less than the Badshah of Dilli had been apologizing so profusely to him. Touched to the heart, he set off to escort his new friend Alauddin out of Chittor fort.

There was no moon that night and the only light came from the stars. The world lay in darkness. The doors of every home were shut. After a day's hard toil, the people of the city were now asleep. There was not a soul to be seen on the broad avenues of Chittor. Alauddin rode his horse down the empty streets, accompanied by Rana Bhimsingh and twenty Rajput soldiers.

The Rana was feeling very happy. He had made friends with Chittor's greatest enemy, Alauddin. Chittor would now never have to face the repression of Dilli. When he thought of the Pathan army leaving Chittor the next morning, when he imagined how every citizen of Chittor would be able to get on with their lives from the next day without any fear and would hail their king and queen mightily for this, his heart danced with joy. Blissfully riding alongside the Badshah, he came out of Chittor through one of its great gates.

The night was even darker now. The tall tamarind trees on both sides of the mountain path stood like rows of black ogres. The world was silent. The only sounds to be heard were the occasional shouts of the citadel guards and the clip-clop of the hooves of the twenty-two horses.

Having cleverly engaged Bhimsingh in polite chatter, Alauddin had now managed to get him down to the foot of the mountain. On one side were the fields of maize, and on the other the mango orchard. Ahead lay a rough road.

The two hundred Pathan soldiers who had been hiding in the orchard, as planned by Alauddin, surrounded Bhimsingh as soon as he appeared. They were two hundred and the Rajputs only twenty. The Rajputs fought fearlessly to save their Rana, but it was of no use. Just as a falcon swoops down and picks up its prey, Alauddin's Pathans captured Bhimsingh from within his protective circle of warriors.

Only five of the twenty Rajput soldiers returned to Chittor. At first light of the first day of the fortnight when the moon waxes to its full glory, the news spread all over Chittor – Bhimsingh was now a prisoner and would not be freed till he gave up Padmini to the Badshah.

Alauddin had reached his camp in the dead of night. He ordered Bhimsingh to be imprisoned securely and went to his grand tent to rest. He now firmly believed that since the Rana had been captured there was no way Padmini could escape him. Hindu women were willing to sacrifice their lives for their husbands – why would Padmini not agree to be a begum of the Badshah? He would never release the Rana unless he got Padmini.

Having made this resolution, Alauddin lay on the soft sheets as white as milk foam in his bed of gold and fell asleep when dawn was about to break, thinking of Rani Padmini.

It was morning. Padmini would arrive any time now, thought the Badshah. But the morning wore on to afternoon and then evening came, and there was no sign of Padmini. The Badshah grew restless. He even began wondering if the man he had captured was the right Bhimsingh! Had he kidnapped only some minor warlord? He ordered the prisoner to be produced before him. Bound in iron chains, Rana Bhimsingh faced Alauddin in his durbar like a shackled lion. 'Are you Padmini's Bhimsingh?' asked the Shahenshah.

'Pathan, why do you have doubts about that?' asked Bhimsingh.

'If you are truly Bhimsingh,' said Alauddin, 'then why do I see no effort from your loyal Rajputs to free you?'

'Maybe the Maharana of Chittor does not care to maintain any relations with a fool who, due to his own delusions, ended up being a prisoner of lying enemies,' said Bhimsingh.

This raised disquiet in the Badshah's mind. What if the king of Chittor had actually abandoned Bhimsingh and was going to let him stay a prisoner? Worried, Alauddin got up and left the durbar.

As that night gave way to dawn, Padmini stood alone on the terrace of the citadel of Chittor, deep in thought. Her two lovely eyes turned their gaze on the Pathan camp where Bhimsingh lay imprisoned. The sky was still murky, and on the east the light from the sun was just a few arrows of gold when two Rajput chieftains came and knelt before her. One was called Gora, the other Baadal. Gora was fifty years old and Baadal, son of Gora's elder brother, only twelve.

Both belonged to Padmini's parental clan. When she left Sinhala to become Bhimsingh's queen, Gora had come with her to Chittor, in his hand a sword and in his lap Baadal, the orphan baby. 'Has the Maharana agreed to act as per my advice?' asked Padmini.

'By his order, I am now going to meet the Badshah to make arrangements for sending the Rani to the camp of the Pathans,' said Gora.

Padmini smiled a faint smile. 'Go tell the Badshah that he must build a new palace in Dilli to welcome me when I come.'

Gora and Baadal left. Soon Suryadev rose, lighting up the whole world. Padmini watched as the rays of the morning sun turned the red silk canopies of Alauddin's massive camp into blood crimson. She looked at the grand tent of the Badshah and said to herself: 'You sly villain, the war between you and me starts today. Let us see who is stronger.'

It was a Friday, the holy day of the Muslims. Alauddin had just sat down at his durbar after completing his special namaz when Gora and Baadal arrived with a letter from the Maharana. The Badshah opened the Maharana's seal on the envelope and began to read it:

> We have decided to hand over Rani Padmini to the Badshah. In exchange, Rana Bhimsingh must be freed. Also, our queen Padmini cannot go to Dilli like a common woman. The Badshah must arrange that her dear friends can stay with her and serve her forever. In addition, the Badshah must make sure that the Rajput noblewomen who accompany Padmini, the queen of Chittor, to the camp, suffer no insult. For this reason, the Badshah must move all his soldiers to a fair distance from the fort. The final wish of the Maharana is that Alauddin should desist from all enmity with him in the future.

The letter drove the Badshah into an ecstasy. He turned to Gora and Baadal with a broad smile on his face and said: 'This is fine. I shall withdraw my entire army from the fort by nightfall. The queen will have no problems at all in coming here. Go tell your Maharana, I am agreeable to everything that he has said.'

Gora and Baadal left. The Badshah ordered his troops to retreat from the fort. It was not easy to relocate such a huge army quickly and settle it in a new spot. Let the tents and the weaponry and all the paraphernalia stay where they are, commanded Alauddin. The soldiers should use their own horses to retreat and take shelter for a day. But even this operation took nearly the whole night to be carried out.

As the sun rose the next day, drums thundered from the top of Rampal, the main gate of Chittor. The Badshah saw that around seven hundred palanquins, each with four bearers, had passed through the seven gates of the citadel and were coming towards his camp. Right in the middle of the convoy was Rani Padmini's golden palanquin, wrapped in the finest Chinese silk, accompanied on horseback by the fifty-year-old Gora on one side and the twelve-year-old boy Baadal on the other.

The Badshah had laid out canopies over almost two square miles for Padmini and her companions to stay in. When all the seven hundred palanquins had reached the camp, Gora appeared before the Badshah and informed him: 'Shahenshah, the queen is here. She now wishes to meet Bhimsingh, for the two of them will never see each other again after she becomes the Badshah's begum.'

'Who am I to deny Padmini when she desires to meet the Rana?' said Alauddin. 'I grant her half an hour

– the Rana cannot stay longer than that with her.' Gora and Baadal bowed to the Badshah and left.

Alauddin sat alone and watched the seven hundred palanquins emerge from under the canopies and travel towards Chittor. The twelve-year-old Baadal was riding his horse with them. 'Who goes in all these palanquins?' the Badshah asked one of his noblemen. He was told that all the women from the aristocratic Rajput families who had come to bid the queen farewell were now returning home. 'Where is Bhimsingh?' he asked. 'He is inside, with Padmini,' came the reply.

Alauddin looked at the sand dial in a corner of his tent and saw that the stipulated half hour had passed. Now he would be able to meet Padmini. He walked over to another tent where he stored all his finery. Here it was all perfume and roses and gems – little bowls of gold filled with rose water that cost a thousand coins a drop, caps made of pearls, emerald-studded fabrics to be wound around the head, boxes filled with diamond rings, priceless muslin garments hanging from the shelves, countless silk handkerchiefs and casual shrugs woven from silver threads.

While the Badshah stood before his mirror, now dressed in his best regalia, with a scarf of woven silver round his neck and shoulders, and perfumed his greying beard with the distilled essence of rose, elite Rajput chieftains were taking the seven hundred palanquins, with Rana Bhimsingh hidden in one of them, back to Chittor from the Pathan camp.

At last Alauddin was finished with his dressing up. The half-hour was long over. It was close to an hour now, but Bhimsingh had not returned from Padmini's camp. The Badshah called for Gora but he was nowhere to be found. Alauddin could not stay in his tent any longer. He hurried to the two-square-mile canopy that had been erected for the Rajput ladies. Padmini's golden palanquin lay there, empty. The huge tent of maroon velvet that he had built, where he had hoped to keep Padmini the queen of Chittor as his pet, like a golden bird in a gem-encrusted cage, was deserted and dark.

Where was Padmini and her hundreds of friends, and where was the prisoner Bhimsingh? There was an uproar all over the camp. Everyone had now come to realize that Rajput warriors had come dressed as palanquin bearers, fooled them all and rescued the Rana.

At once the Badshah ordered his army to get ready and rode off towards Chittor with two thousand horsemen.

The Rana's palanquin had only just entered the fort when the Badshah's cavalry descended on the Rajput soldiers like a desert storm. Fierce battle cries pierced the air and the clouds of dust raised by the horses' hooves darkened the sky.

It was high noon now. Under the fiery blaze of the sun, the twelve-year-old Baadal and the fifty-year-old Gora, along with a platoon of Rajputs, defended the main gate of Chittor without a care for their lives. Evening fell, but the battle continued. Hundreds and hundreds of Rajputs came out of the fort and joined the battle. The Badshah brought in thousands of Pathans but could not even scratch a single stone of the walls of Chittor. Finally, when Bhimsingh, the man whom he had put in iron chains, arrived at the battlefield, riding an elephant, all hope and confidence that the Badshah had had vanished.

In the half dark of dusk, Alauddin, emperor of half of Bharat, turned his horse around from Chittor and went back to his camp. Joyful cries of victory resounded all through the fort.

Late that night, Rana Bhimsingh came to Padmini's bedroom to rest. Seeing that he had tears in his eyes, Padmini asked: 'Why do you weep on such a happy day?' The Rana sighed. 'Padmini, our always-faithful

Gora left the game of war forever today and ascended to the realm of the gods,' he said. The two did not speak another word. Padmini blew out the lamps. All through the night the wind from the south seemed to carry into the room the sound of wails from the great cremation ground of Chittor.

While Alauddin had been sitting in siege outside Chittor, an army of the Mughals had been advancing slowly from Kabul towards Bharat. When the Badshah returned to camp after his defeat at the hands of the Rajputs, he heard that the Mughal king Taimurlane was coming to attack Dilli.

He also received a letter from Piyari Begum: 'Shahenshah,' she had written. 'How much longer? Please let go of your hope for Padmini. While you, like a honeybee, wandered around the deserts to look for a lotus, a bear came out of the jungle and looted your hive. It is all the will of Allah. Today one is the emperor of half of Bharat, and tomorrow that same man can be a beggar on the streets. Alas! Perhaps Piyari Begum of Dilli will now have to be a slave woman of Mughal bandits.'

The Badshah was dumbfounded. He had never imagined that the danger was so serious and so close. He immediately ordered the dismantling of the camp.

That night the Pathans left Rajasthan and set off for Kashmir.

~

Thirteen years later, the war drums of the Badshah beat once more before Chittor. The conditions there were very bad at the time. The kingdom had been ravaged by famines and epidemics. Almost all the great warriors were gone. The men in charge of the army were young and inexperienced. Rana Bhimsingh, with his new army and new commanders, fought the Pathans at every step, in every village, on every road. But all his efforts were in vain.

Alauddin defeated the Rajputs in battle after battle and captured village after village and fortress after fortress. Rana Bhimsingh failed to stop the onslaught. The Badshah now stood once again at the gates of Chittor fort. His army set up a citadel-like camp on the mountain to the south of Chittor and prepared for its last war against the Rajputs. The Badshah had pledged that he would not return to Dilli until he had razed Chittor to the ground.

Lakshmansingh called Bhimsingh to the royal court and said: 'Uncle, it seems that Chittor will finally be captured by the Pathans. There does not appear to be any way out. All our subjects are desolate and in great pain. The whole land is being devastated by famine, and now this new threat. How will we fight them, and with whom?'

'Chittor still has great warriors,' replied Bhimsingh. 'We have the capacity to battle the Pathans for a year.'

Lakshmansingh shook his head. 'Uncle, going to war again will be futile,' he said. 'I have realized that unless we seek a truce with the Pathans, we will not survive. Why then should we light the fire of war in this time of grave famine? All our subjects are relying on me. If my loss brings peace back to the land, if the fires are doused, then what is wrong with seeking a truce? Perhaps I can spend the rest of my years peacefully as a vassal of the Badshah.'

Bhimsingh's eyes welled up with tears. He grasped the Maharana's hands. 'Alas Lachhman, I know very well that there is no other way, but I still have one request to make of you,' he said. 'After your parents left this world, when you were only two years old, it was I who had held you to my breast as if you were my own child. I have endured without hesitation all the dangers and all the troubles and worries of running the kingdom, only for you. So please agree to the request

I make today, my son. Give me seven days. Let me try to save Chittor one last time. All I ask for is that we do not call for truce with the Pathans for these seven days, and that, during this period, my commands are obeyed by all as the Maharana's commands.'

'So be it,' said Lakshmansingh.

From that day onwards, as chosen and ordered by Bhimsingh, Rajput chieftains began to go to battle with the Pathans. Every day news would come in of this prince losing his life on the battlefield, of that chieftain taken prisoner by the enemy. Wails and lamentations rose from every home in Chittor. Those lamentations, those cries of grief from thousands of orphaned children and widowed women, reached Padmini as she sat in worship in the marble temple at the centre of the lake of lotus flowers. She completed her puja, but all evening her tender heart wept for those who had lost their loved ones.

When Bhimsingh returned home one night, Padmini folded her hands before him and asked: 'Lord, how much longer will this war continue?' 'Only three more days,' said Bhimsingh. 'But there is nothing to be gained any more, and the hearts of the Rajput soldiers are also flagging in energy. But we have no choice. Now the Maharana of the Sun Dynasty will have to live as a servant of the Pathan Badshah.'

'Lord, is there no way that Chittor can be saved?' asked Padmini.

'Only if Ubar Devi grants us a boon,' said Bhimsingh. 'Oh Padmini, we must have committed some grave sins in our past lives to have reduced Chittor to this terrible state!'

Padmini sat alone in her room in the dark and Bhimsingh's words kept resonating in her head: 'Oh Padmini, we must have committed some grave sins in our past lives to have reduced Chittor to this terrible state!' She hit her forehead hard with her fist. 'Wretched Padmini!' she said to herself. 'It is your accursed beauty that has brought on this calamity – all this is because of you!' The walls of the room seemed to echo her: 'All this is because of you!'

At that very moment, clouds obscured the clear sky of the month of Chaitra and rain began coming down in large, heavy drops. Padmini covered herself with a thick cape and walked down alone from her palace to the temple of Ubar Devi, mother goddess of Chittor.

It was midnight now. All the lamps in the temple had died out and only a single earthen one flickered on. Sitting in that dim light, the devi's bhairavi, the goddess's head priestess and an expert of the occult, told Rani Padmini: 'Maharani, let me tell you once more. What you are trying to do can only end in death. If you wear the devi's jewellery even once there is no escape. Within six months you will be burned alive.'

'Mother,' said Padmini, 'Bless me that my wish is granted – that this accursed beauty that has set Rajasthan on fire may be turned to ashes.'

The bhairavi replied: 'Then let it be so, my daughter. May your name reign eternal in Chittor, for which you are sacrificing your life. May our goddess, who represents the highest womanly virtues and whose jewellery you will wear, accept you lovingly at her feet after your death.' Rani Padmini took all the jewels of the goddess from the bhairavi, placed them in a sandalwood casket and left.

It was the dead of night. There was not a sound to be heard anywhere in the royal palace of Chittor. The Maharana sat alone in a hall. All his subjects had gone to sleep, relieved that he would make peace with the Pathans. But Maharana Lakshmansingh, Regent of Ekalinga, was unable to sleep. Cruel fate seemed to have decreed that he would have to leave Chittor the next day, once the peace treaty was signed. He would perhaps never be able to come back. He would have to spend the rest of his life in exile in some faraway land as a mere commoner, having forfeited his kingdom, his status, his honour and all his dear ones.

He sighed and looked at the golden lamp holder in a corner of the room. Only one lamp still burned. The rest of the enormous chamber was totally dark. The rows of pillars and doorways seemed to be melding into an even deeper black. In the light of that solitary lamp, the great dead silent hall was more dark than dark could be. It was an abyss. The Maharana got up to go to his bedroom.

And then, suddenly – could it be that the stones of the floor trembled at the sound of footsteps for a moment? The Maharana thought he could smell the fragrance of many flowers and hear the soft *jhini-jhini* of many anklets. Who were these people moving around in the dark? 'Who are you? What do you want?' shouted the Maharana.

From deep inside the walls of the hall, from above its roof, from below the king's feet, from all around him, a voice rose and reverberated – '*Main bhookhi hoon*' – I am hungry. 'Who is still awake in the garden of the royal palace of Chittor?' asked Lakshmansingh. The reply came – the same three words once more: 'I am hungry.' And then, just as a dream takes slow shape within deep slumber, a magnificent goddess began to appear from the all-surrounding blackness.

'Whoever you are, god or demon, why are you trying

to trick me?' cried Lakshmansingh. He took the golden lamp from the lamp stand and raised it high. The light from that solitary lamp blazed like a thousand flames as it fell on the countless jewels that adorned the goddess, from her head to her feet. Lakshmansingh could now see the mother goddess who ruled Chittor, Ubar Devi, the empress of all.

The Maharana was paralysed with fear, wonder and devotion. The golden lamp fell from his hands, which were now shaking from both dread and ecstasy. Then all was dark. In that darkness the Maharana could not even comprehend whether he was awake or dreaming.

He only seemed to keep hearing those words: 'I am hungry. Deeply hungry, deeply thirsty – I need a great sacrifice. Only blood can quench my thirst. Maharana, wake up, rise, shed the blood of your breast for your land. Let my blood flow as hundreds of rivulets and streams and rivers and fulfil me. Chittor can only be saved if every boy and every old man pledges to give up his life for our land. Otherwise the kings of the Suryavamsha will never get their kingdom back from the Pathans.'

Like an echo bouncing endlessly off the walls of deep mountain caves, the last words of the goddess continued to resound all around the Maharana.

The night ended. The goddess-empress of Chittor had vanished in the golden light and cool breeze of the dawn. From the temple of Parvati far away came the sound of devotional songs set to Bhairavi, the raga that celebrates sunrise.

When Lakshmansingh revealed the events of the night and the goddess's commands to the royal court, they were stunned, though there were many who did not believe him. But those with unshakable faith and resolve, and who were ready to give up their lives for Chittor, were energized to the point of frenzy. Others, whose hearts lacked passion and whose minds were frail – those who had been thinking that they could live a peaceful and content life if peace were made with the Pathans – turned sullen and sad.

However, that night, the Maharana invited all the chieftains of Mewar to his personal chamber to see if the devi would appear again. The goddess manifested in all her fearsome splendour out of the darkness once more at midnight before thousands of Rajput warriors and repeated: '*Main bhookhi hoon*' – I am hungry.

There was no doubt left in anyone's mind after this. All scepticism, all weakness, disappeared in an instant, just as darkness evaporates in the brilliance of a blazing fire. A new spirit of courage and defiance intoxicated everyone.

Only Bhimsingh's mind was in turmoil. He thought he had seen Padmini in the figure of the goddess. He kept asking himself: Was this phantom the goddess herself, or was it Padmini? Padmini, or the devi?

Preparations began for the final great sacrifice. Maharana Lakshmansingh placed the golden crown of Chittor on the head of Arisingh, the eldest of his twelve sons, and said: 'O blessed one, follow the commands of the goddess. Go forth against the Pathans. Today, you are the Maharana of all Mewar. Know all these brave chieftains as your subjects. If you win, your prize will be the throne of Chittor in this life. If you die on the battlefield, you will live forever at the feet of the great goddess, where there is nothing to fear.'

The elderly Lakshmansingh stepped down from the throne and stood under it as the crown sparkled on the head of the new king. The shouts went up all over: 'Victory to the Mahadevi! Victory to Arisingh!'

Lakshmansingh turned to the court. 'All my sardars, I have a final duty to perform,' he said. 'This is not a duty to the goddess, nor a duty to Chittor. It is to my ancestors, the Maharanas, who have passed on to the next world. To make sure that the royal family of Mewar is not wiped out in this great war, that all my departed ancestors always find a cupped palm bearing water offered to them whenever they feel thirst, that Bappaditya's dynasty stays immortal through countless eons, it is my wish that prince Ajaysingh, with his wife and children, go to the secluded and safe fort of Kailur.'

Ajaysingh rose. Folding his hands before the Maharana, he said: 'Father, all my eleven brothers will give their lives in battle for Chittor, and I, like a woman, will sit around and nurture my children? Am I so weak, so unworthy?'

'Do not despair, son,' said Lakshmansingh. 'Any true Rajput of Chittor would have felt honoured to be given the noble task that I have burdened you with. The shedding of our blood may not save Chittor. Maybe one day you too will have to stake your life for this land. Maybe we shall leave Chittor in shackles, and maybe you will find a capable knight one day on whom you can bestow the responsibilities of the Dynasty of the Sun and move on from this world in peace. Remember always, there is joy in giving up one's life for Chittor, but the joy of restoring Chittor to its glory will be a hundred times greater.'

Lakshmansingh fell silent. The court was dismissed amid happy cries of '*Jai Jai!*'

As he was bidding farewell to the court, Arisingh told Ajaysingh: 'Meet me before you leave Chittor.'

After he had finalized preparations for his journey, Ajaysingh went to his elder brother's home. Arisingh had just finished writing a letter. 'Brother,' he said, 'this is perhaps the last time we will see each other. Tomorrow, you will be in one world and I in another. On this last day, I want to give you a task.' He pressed a leather pouch into Ajaysingh's hand and the letter he had just written. 'Please take care of these two things,' he said. 'If I return alive from the war, I shall ask you to give them back to me. If I do not, read the letter to know what my last wish is. And give the dagger in the pouch to my son Hambir when he grows up.' He then embraced Ajay and said: 'Come, bhai, let us go and say goodbye to our mother.'

As night paled into dawn and the two princes departed the palace in two different directions, the Maharani of Chittor, mother of twelve sons, threw herself on the floor. Her entire body was as numb as the cold stones of the floor; her two tearful and tormented eyes kept gazing at the door by which the princes had left. 'Dearest,' said the Maharana. 'Still your heart, have patience, keep your resolve. Accept the harsh decree of Time with bowed head and serenity.' And then the war drums of the Rajputs shook the earth and the heavens, and Arisingh rode out to battle.

A month passed. All efforts by the Rajputs against the Pathans came to naught. One by one, all the eleven princes died on the battlefield. There was no hope any more, nor any choice left. Yet the valiant hearts of the Rajputs stayed staunch.

Now the last two great warriors of Chittor, Lakshmansingh and Bhimsingh, prepared for their final battle. At the command of the Maharana, those who remained of the hundreds of thousands of soldiers whom the chieftains had commanded now came together. These were the special ten thousand – the fearsome elite force that owed allegiance to Ekalinga.

In one hand, they carried a lance, in the other an axe. They wore spiral earrings carved from the purest conch shell, their death-black hair was tied in a bun at the top of their heads. Round their necks hung a necklace of rudrakshas, the holy beads of dried stone fruit. Their shoulders were draped in tiger skin and on their backs they carried an enormous shield. Their only earthly possessions were a horse, a blanket and a brass vessel to carry water in. Among the gods they worshipped only Ekalinga, and among mortals they obeyed only the Maharana.

Samarsingh had created this battalion. They were never seen in any ordinary battle. They appeared in the fort of Chittor only when the kingdom was in grave peril, surrounded by the enemy on all sides, when all the women of the land – be they maiden or widow, a ten-year-old child or a sixteen-year-old in the full bloom of youth – fearing they would be defiled by barbarians, fulfilled the last pledge of their lives by hurling themselves into the conflagration of the Jauhar and reducing their bodies and beauty to ashes before the goddess-empress of Chittor. The fearless and ferocious soldiers of the Regent of Ekalinga appeared only when all hope was lost, all choices gone. They heralded the final festival of blood that despairing Rajputs had to revel in.

Seventy years ago, Karma Devi, Rana Samarsingh's widow, had gathered together all the soldiers of Mewar to guard her son's throne from Qutubuddin, the king of Dilli. That was the time when Ekalinga's battalion had last been called upon to fight. Now, several generations later, at the command of Maharana Lakshmansingh, they had arrived again at the fort of Chittor.

It was night and the utter blackness seemed to have swallowed the whole world, as if the sun, the moon and the stars had all died. Now began the Jauhar of twelve thousand magnificent Rajput women at the temple of the goddess-empress, at the great cremation ground of Chittor.

Right in front of the temple, standing at the mouth of a dark tunnel, Rani Padmini, the most beautiful woman in all of Chittor, started her chant to Agni, the god of fire. 'O Agni,' she said, 'O sacred radiant one, come! Let the darkness of this world be banished by your light. O Agni, the most fierce of all gods, come. You are strength for the powerless and support for the powerful. Come, terrifying one, and take away all our fears and regrets and give us shelter. You, defender of our honour, rescuer of us from all our woes, you, the flame divine, you are the final redeemer of our lives who will liberate us from all shackles and attachments.'

Padmini fell silent. Twelve thousand Rajput women danced around the well of fire and sang: 'He who saves our honour! He who protects us from evil!' And then, with a great roar, thousands of flames, as if in a state of primal ecstasy, burst forth from the tunnel under that well. The night itself seemed to tremble and shudder in the face of that intense light. Along with the twelve thousand Rajput women, Rani Padmini plunged into the well. In the blink of an eye all the lovely faces, all the sweet chatter, all the innocent laughter in every home in Chittor turned to ashes.

A cry rose from deep inside the heart of every Rajput man: 'Hail the queen, the most virtuous of all!' Even

Alauddin, reclining in his tent at the bottom of the mountain, could hear it. He immediately ordered all his troops to prepare for battle.

The next day, as soon as the sun rose, Rajput soldiers came down from the mountain of Chittor like a monsoon torrent, shaking the earth with battle cries that invoked Lord Shiva, and fell upon the Pathans with a terrible force.

The Tartar soldiers of Alauddin were no match for the axes of the Ekalinga troops. In a matter of moments they were overpowered and fled for their lives. The Badshah kept sending in new forces, but every effort of his failed – it was like trying to build a dam out of sand to stem a mighty river in full spate.

Alauddin himself was not some minor warrior. He had conquered kingdoms much larger than Mewar with armies much smaller than the one he had brought here. But today, seeing the valour of the Rajputs, he felt fear. Twelve times he arranged his forces and sent them to fight, and twelve times he had to retreat. He understood that this battle would not end easily. Which one of the two would stay, and which would fall? The power of the Badshah of Dilli or the throne of Chittor?

As evening approached, Alauddin ordered his entire army to advance all at once on the ten thousand Rajputs.

Hundreds of thousands of the Badshah's soldiers, horses and elephants charged the Rajputs like demons, raising a storm of sand and dust that turned day into night. And then, like the stream of a river meeting the waves of an ocean, the few thousand Rajputs who were fighting vanished somewhere in the midst of the countless Pathan troops, and no one could see them any more. The royal flag of Chittor, with the sign of Suryadev on it, rose over the heads of all the battling men, glittering like a streak of lightning in the glow of the setting sun one last time, and then it was gone. Immediately after came the shouts of victory: '*Allah hu Akbar!* Victory to the Badshah!'

All the insignias of the Maharana were crushed under the feet of the Pathans. The sun went down, shrouding the world in darkness. Swarms of ravenous nightbirds spread their black wings and flew around the battlefield, looking for carrion. Chittor had been captured.

Pathan swords bathed the streets of Chittor in blood. The coffers of the hundreds of thousands of Tartar soldiers were filled to bursting with coins and gold and gems and jewellery. But . . .

Alauddin had left the throne of Dilli, come to a foreign land and turned the city of Chittor, as magnificent as the kingdom of the gods, into a vast funeral pyre . . . all because of his lust for one jewel. But at the end of it all, did he find that jewel?

As soon as the Badshah entered Chittor, he came to know that Padmini was no more – only ashes remained of the beautiful flower he had tried so desperately to own.

That night, on orders from the Badshah, every standing building in Chittor – home or palace, temple or monastery – was either demolished or burnt down. Only Rani Padmini's marble temple at the centre of the huge lake of lotus flowers remained untouched and glowing. Alauddin rested for three days in her bedroom with its marble verandas that overlooked the lake and the royal temple. Then he gave a Rajput called Maldev charge of Chittor's administration and began a slow journey back to Dilli.

The power of the Pathan Badshah spread from one end of Hindustan to the other. But the sacred names of the twelve thousand virtuous Rajput women and the glorious tales of the valour of thousands of Rajput warriors became immortal. Even today one can see Padmini's well of fire. But none can enter there – a giant python lies in guard all day and night at the mouth of the abyss.

5

Hambir

Chittor had not yet been captured by the Pathans. Rana Bhimsingh held complete sway over Mewar, administering the kingdom on behalf of his nephew Maharana Lakshmansingh. One day, during this period of peace, happiness and prosperity in the land, crown prince Arisingh went on a hunt with his friends.

The group of huntsmen, along with the prince, was chasing its prey – a pointy-faced wild boar with huge tusks – down an earthen track near the village of Ujala by the Andhoa forest. But at high noon, after a long run that blew up huge clouds of dust along the path, the prince's target plunged into a maize field on the side of the track. The horses could not go in there, and arrows were useless.

Standing on a makeshift bamboo machan high in

the middle of the field, a Rajput girl was watching the fun. She wore a blue dress and had a yellow scarf covering her head. The prince had a long green piece of the most expensive muslin wrapped around his neck. Their eyes met.

Later, when the prince, disappointed with his failure to get his prey, was riding to the mango orchard by the Bunas river, the girl appeared again. She had killed the boar and had dragged the carcass through the field to offer it as a gift to the hunters.

'How did you kill it?' asked the prince.

The girl showed him a reed of maize as straight and sharp as a spear and replied: 'I impaled it with this.' Her dust-laden pitch-black hair circled her beautiful face like the hoods of a hundred serpents. The brass bangles on her supple wrists glittered like gold in the sunlight as she went on her way.

The prince rested in the cool shade of the mango trees by the Bunas. He kept thinking about the girl and soon he began to doze off.

One does not know whether the girl too was thinking of the prince as she returned to her field and got busy chasing away birds and goats from the crop by throwing lumps of earth at them. But one lump slipped from her fingers and went flying in the wrong direction, landing at the feet of the prince's horse standing by the mango orchard. The prince woke up with a start at the neigh of his stallion. Through a gap in the trees he could see a slice of the maize field, and there in the middle of it was the peasant girl with her yellow scarf and blue dress.

The field of pigeon peas rippled in waves in the west wind, a flock of parrots was flying overhead, the light was fading as the day came to an end, and the sky was as clear and still as a vast slab of marble with just a few thin lines of black cloud on it as the prince set off for home. And then the two saw each other again, by the side of the river where the path that ran through the field met the village track. The girl was carrying a vessel of milk on her head; with her were two buffalo calves, their skin black as the softest velvet.

The next day, an emissary of the prince arrived at the girl's home in Ujala village with a proposal of marriage. But the girl's father, a Chauhan Rajput of the Chandosa clan, flatly refused to give his daughter's hand in marriage to a Gahlot. The crestfallen prince returned to his kingdom. But there was no end to the criticism and jeering that the elderly Rajput and his wife now faced from their neighbours, friends and kinspeople. How could he do such a thing? What sort of a man pushes away Lakshmi, Goddess of Prosperity, with his feet? Ah well, they said, if he doesn't have even this much sense, he deserves to stay a poor peasant forever.

The father had only one reply to all the jibes: 'You can go ahead and say whatever you like, but I cannot send off my Lachhmi to be the maidservant of five other wives in a king's palace. It is far better that she be the sole housewife in charge of a poor man's home.'

But the old man's resolve did not last too long. A messenger arrived from Rani Padmini. 'I have no children,' she had written. 'I beg you for your daughter. May the mother goddess of Chittor welcome your family into our fold with my blessings.'

The words of a virtuous woman do not go in vain. There remained no doubt now that Lachhmi's son would one day sit on the throne of Chittor. With glorious pageantry that lit up the skies, the prince, dressed in the grandest of bridegroom finery on his splendidly decorated horse, came to the village of Ujala, like a man descended from a kingdom of dreams. For everyone in the village, it was a night of great celebration, joy, song and dance. All that they could recall afterwards was that it was a festival of the sweetest love and delight.

A year passed. The crown prince came to Ujala with Rani Lachhmi and their one-month-old son Hambir. He left them in the village and went to fight the Pathans. No Rajput returned from that war. The Rana, the princes, Bhimsingh, Rani Padmini, the royal daughters-in-law, the king's mother . . . all perished. The mother-goddess of Chittor seemed to have abandoned her domain. The only ones who remained of the royal family were Rani Lachhmi in Ujala with the infant Hambir, and in the fortress of Kailur, Ajaysingh, the sole surviving son of Rana Lakshmansingh.

The ancient fortress of Kailur was on a hill nestled between a little village called Shoronal and the Aravalli mountains. It had been built long ago to keep an eye on the Bhils who lived in the mountains. There used to be a time when the Maharanas of Chittor would spend four months of the year there. The fortress had been a magnificent one, but after the mountain tribes were subdued and forsook enmity to accept the rule of Chittor, there was little need for the Maharanas to come to Kailur any more. Once in a while a prince or two would arrive for a hunt and spend a night there. Over the decades the fortress fell into disuse, its walls began to crumble, and wild trees and weeds ran riot all over.

Then, on a night of a raging storm, rain and flashing lightning, Lakshmansingh's son Ajaysingh, driven out of his kingdom, came to take shelter in Kailur with his wife and children. It was a terrible night like no other.

Rainwater dripped through the cracks in the ceilings, rats scurried around in the corners of the rooms, bats flapped their wings noisily under the ceiling. The prince and his wife piled some hay on the wet floor and spent the night on that miserable bed, covering themselves with blankets that were meant to keep horses warm.

When in the morning the villagers arrived to meet their king, they saw that he did not have either a throne or a bed. Rana Ajaysingh, who should have been sitting on a throne under a royal canopy, and the queen, who should have been resting on a carved ivory bed with her two princes, Ajimsingh and Sujansingh, were sitting on horse blankets. Immediately, the villagers began to clean up the fortress with care and zeal and started decorating the rooms.

The richest landowner in the village brought a throne and a bed of ivory, velvet couches, a canopy woven out of gold thread, sandalwood fans, silver lamps, and utensils of carved gold and marble. From the fields the peasant girls brought vegetables, vessels filled with ghee, milch cows and grass for the horses to eat. In no time the fortress was back to its former splendour. In the evening the villagers left the palace, and there were smiles on the faces of the king, the queen and the two boy princes.

The tremendous efforts by the loyal villagers to

make them comfortable helped Ajaysingh forget all his sorrows, except for one that would never leave him – that Chittor was now under Pathan rule. He would often lament with a deep sigh: 'Alas! The sun is still in eclipse, and no one knows when it will shine again. How long will I have to wait?'

Years passed. But the day of glory that Ajaysingh pined for never arrived. He was prepared to give his life to take Chittor back from the Pathans, but he had neither the men nor the money to accomplish this. He had hoped fervently that the two princes, Ajimsingh and Sujansingh, would try to liberate their father's kingdom, but the gods dashed that dream too.

It was monsoon and the rain clouds had cast shadows as black as kohl on the peaks of the Aravalli mountains. Light and shadow played hide-and-seek with each other above the village and the fields. The two princes had gone out to hunt, and the king and queen were alone at home.

Evening came but the princes had not returned. The queen kept looking out of the open windows. Soon Suryadev splashed a little golden wave on the western sky and retreated below the horizon. The clouds turned darker and made the night even more black. The queen was speaking to the king, but she would glance out of the window every once in a while.

'You seem distracted today,' said the king.

'I don't know why, but my heart is quaking,' said the queen and left the room. A maid came in with lamps. The rain pattered, *tup-taap*, in big, heavy drops.

The queen returned with an ashen face. 'Our sons went off on their hunt in the morning,' she said. 'Why haven't they come back yet?'

'What? They haven't returned?' said the Rana. 'Where could they be, in all this rain and storm?' As he spoke, a commotion rose in the courtyard of the fortress. The clouds had now receded and the moon had risen. The king and queen saw that some villagers were carrying someone in. A maid rushed in and said: 'Rani-Ma, come and see what has happened to our Ajimsingh Bahadur!' A moment later the men brought the prince into the room.

The king and queen learnt that up in the mountains, Sujansingh had got into an argument with the son of the Bhil chieftain Munja over some issue about who had actually killed a deer, and the dispute had soon turned into a fight. Ajimsingh had been badly wounded in the head when he tried to defend his brother. 'And where is Sujansingh now?' asked the Rana.

The villagers scratched their heads and said: 'He is well. He sent us off. He is resting at an inn and should be coming here any time now.'

The Rana knew very well that resting at a roadside inn for Sujansingh meant hanging out with friends and getting drunk on siddhi, a concoction of milk and marijuana. 'It's not advisable to rest during a time of danger,' he said.

The visitors left. The king, the queen, the royal physician and a few maids stayed with the unconscious Ajim. The prince did not regain his senses that night. 'It's a dreadful wound,' said the physician, shaking his head. As dawn broke, the prince opened his eyes for a moment. He called out once for his mother, and then, just as a bird that has escaped its cage flies away, the life force left the prince's golden body.

Time went by. Grief and despair ate away at Ajaysingh and he became more dejected by the day. Meanwhile, that ferocious bandit Munja grew ever-more powerful and began tyrannizing the villagers and all of Ajaysingh's subjects. One night this brigand even reached the fortress of Kailur and looted it. He snatched Ajaysingh's crown away, struck him on the head with his sword and left.

Ajaysingh was now old and Sujansingh the prince was a drug addict. Who would protect the people? On one side were the raids by the Pathans; on the other Munja's cruel repression. And then rumour spread that

Ajaysingh did not have very long to live. The people of the kingdom wept and lamented. Everyone began to say that the glory of the Suryavamsha was now over. No one believed that Sujan Bahadur could run the state.

At this time, when the kingdom was in such dire straits, Rani Lachhmi arrived at Kailur from the village of Ujala with her son Hambir. All the friends and relatives of the Rana and all the chieftains were present in Rana Ajaysingh's court that morning when Hambir entered and touched the Rana's feet. The Rana blessed him and sat him down close to himself.

As he looked at Hambir, he could almost see his eldest brother Arisingh. Hambir had the same nose as his father, and the same eyes; the same fine, powerful body and the same deep but sweet voice. Ajaysingh suddenly remembered that before leaving for his last battle against the Pathans, Arisingh had given him a leather pouch and a letter. He had told him that the letter contained his last wishes and that Ajaysingh should hand over the dagger in the pouch to Hambir when he came of age.

Now Rana Ajaysingh handed over Arisingh's dagger and the letter with the late Rana's personal seal on it to Hambir as all the chieftains watched. He said: 'Dear boy, read what your father's last wishes were.'

Arisingh had written:

Hail Sri Ram
With the blessings of Sri Ganesha
With the blessings of Ma Kali
By the order of Arisingh, King of Kings:

My command to Ajaysingh-ji and all the chieftains and citizens of the ten thousand cantons of Mewar is that if, by the wishes of Ma Bhavani, I lose my life in the war against the Pathans, then, as per the custom of our land, my brother Ajaysingh shall assume the mantle of the Regent of Ekalinga and govern the kingdom and take care of all its subjects.

To ensure a comfortable life for my widow Rani Lachhmi and our little child Hambir, he shall arrange to transfer the village of Ujala and its surrounding lands to the name of the queen. Thus, I transfer the Regency on the basis of my knowledge and faith. However, the day may come when there is a dispute between Hambir and the sons of my brother over inheriting the throne. Therefore, it is my last request that the man who assumes the Regency of Ekalinga after Ajaysingh-ji should be the person whom our chieftains and ministers and citizens decide is the right candidate for this responsibility.

> It is my command to Hambir and the other princes that they should not enter into any quarrel over the inheritance. Our land is in great peril and an internal conflict is not desirable. May Ekalinga's curse strike those among our descendants who indulge in such conflicts.
>
> – Samvat 1333, Chittorgarh.

After the letter had been read aloud in court, Rana Ajaysingh said: 'We now know what our duty is. All the chieftains of the land are present here. My desire is that this assembly should decide between Sujan Bahadur and Hambir. I know that I do not have much time left on this earth. So I wish to hand over the responsibility of the Regency to the right person while I am still alive. I would like all of you to decide which of the two princes is right for the throne.'

A ferocious debate began in the court. And this was when Sujansingh – large-bellied, with drug-addled eyes bloodshot and only half open – entered the hall. The court was now split into two.

One side said that Sujan Bahadur should get the throne because one needs physical prowess to run a state and everyone knew that the prince had great physical strength. The other side said: How can only physical prowess be enough? One needs patience and intelligence to run a state, and Sujan Bahadur has neither of these qualities. The army is what gives a king his strength. If the king has to go himself and fight battles, what were they for? They said Hambir should be made king.

The first side said: Brothers, the times are bad – merely sitting on the throne with a crown on your head is of little use. We need to go to war. We want a king who can single-handedly stop a hundred Pathans.

The dispute continued till it seemed as if the two sides would come to blows.

Finally Rana Ajaysingh intervened. 'Please calm down and listen to what I have to say,' he said. 'All of you know that just the other day the Bhil leader Munja had come and looted this fortress and we could do nothing about it. That night the bandit absconded with the royal crown of Mewar. As if this were not enough, I have received news that he now wears the crown on his head and is going around saying that he is the king of Rajasthan. There can be only one way to redress this grave insult to the Sun Dynasty – recover the crown.'

'Both Hambir and Sujan are deserving of the throne,' he continued. 'Let the one who can bring back the crown along with the head of that evil creature Munja be my successor. I want the head of that ingrate Bhil who has dared to wear the crown of Mewar brought to me quickly, otherwise I will find no peace even in death. And if the crown of Mewar cannot be recovered by our two able princes, I shall know that the Suryavamsha – the Dynasty of the Sun God – is over; that there is not one valiant warrior left in the land, and that it would be better if it were ruled by Bhils and Pathans. The two princes can use all the soldiers and all the weapons we have in the fortress in whichever way they want to. The court is dismissed.'

The next day, by the time the sun rose, Sujan Bahadur had set off with his friends and cohorts and the entire army of Kailur to catch the dacoits. He had been very busy. On other days he did not wake up before eleven in the morning, but that day he had got ready even before dawn broke. In fact, he had been so busy that he had found no time to ask Hambir to go with him. The elder prince left the fortress while most of its people were still asleep.

'The young prince didn't come?' asked a few chieftains. Sujansingh smirked. 'Oh, he's resting a bit,' he said. 'Let us go forth. He can come after he has had his breakfast.'

At once a toady courtier said: 'Yes, let us go first and surround the bandits' den, and then the junior prince can come and cut his head off.' Another said: 'The Rana is losing his marbles in his old age. This is not something that can be done by just any ordinary man. You need the heart of a lion. This is not your usual dacoit – this is Munja. The whole land trembles in fear when they hear his name, and our junior prince is going to catch him? That's like hoping that an ant can kill an elephant!' And the son of some minister commented: 'No, no, you don't understand the way a king's mind works. Use one thorn to get rid of another, that's what this is.'

Sujansingh laughed. 'You people don't know, but Hambir is very strong,' he said. 'But he's still a kid with no experience at all. When I come back from battle, I'll arrange for him to get lessons in some real wrestling.'

Meanwhile, Hambir had woken up and was sharpening an old sword and a dagger on a whetstone. The dagger was the one his father Arisingh had left for him and the sword had been gifted to him by his grandfather in Ujala village. Today the weapons were tasting a whetstone after many years, and like a river current fed by the rains, were becoming razor-sharp once more. As he sat honing the weapons, Rani Lachhmi came to him and asked: 'What are you doing sitting here?'

'Don't you know, Ma?' said Hambir. 'I have to go and catch that dacoit, so I'm sharpening my weapons.'

'Curse my fate!' said Rani Lachhmi. 'You're still sharpening your sword and dagger, and in the meantime Sujansingh has gone off with all the soldiers. You foolish boy, he seems to be much more competent than you. Now I know that those nasty stories that people spread about him are all lies.'

Hambir was surprised. 'Ma, he didn't ask me to go with him?' he said. 'I suppose being king is not in my destiny. But I'm not giving up.' And he began working on the weapons with double the enthusiasm.

'Get up, get up,' said the queen. 'It's late already – go and eat something. Let me sharpen these two weapons while you go and eat.' Hambir left to have breakfast. Rani Lachhmi sat down with the sword and dagger. A Rajput woman is more expert at honing sabres than at grinding spices and chopping vegetables. In no time the weapons were spotless and shining.

When Hambir returned, Rani Lachhmi handed him the dagger and said: 'There seems to be a crack in this. I can see a wavy line of something on it. This is not going to be of any use.'

'How can you think, Ma, that my father's dagger is of no use?' said Hambir. He turned the dagger round in the light several times and examined it, but could not be sure. A line seemed to straggle from one end of it to the other, but there was no way to know if it was a crack or dried blood.

'Strange,' said Hambir. 'I can't make out what it is. We'll need to look at it closely. Ma, will you keep these weapons in my room? Let me go and meet the king. I'll need a good horse.'

Ajaysingh had not gone to his court that day. He was feeling unwell and was resting in his private quarters. When he saw Hambir coming, he said: 'What, you have not left yet? Sujan went off a long time ago.'

'Sir, I need some time to select a horse,' said Hambir. 'I will certainly start off by evening.'

'All the men have gone with the elder prince,' said Ajaysingh. 'How will you find the way to Munja's lair all by yourself?'

'Sir, I have arranged with a huntsman, he will take me to the bandits' den,' replied Hambir. 'I had initially planned to take soldiers with me, but then I thought about it and decided that it may be impossible to defeat a ferocious and powerful creature like Munja the Bhil in a straight battle. We will have to use guile to accomplish our goal.'

'Do what you think is best,' said Ajaysingh. 'May you be victorious.' Hambir reverently touched his feet and went away.

Hambir was resting in his room when Rani Lachhmi came in and said: 'What's this, why are you lazing in bed? I don't see you making any effort towards going to battle. Are you scared? You told me that you were going to arrange for a horse, and now I find you sleeping!'

'Wait a while, Ma,' said Hambir with a smile. 'It's not an easy job to go and catch a bandit. Let me think for a bit and make a clever plan. Is Munja a wild boar that I can run it through with a reed of maize and drag it back?'

Rani Lachhmi realized that though Hambir spoke in jest, he seemed to have worked out some plan inside his head. 'Oh, so you joke with me?' she said. 'Bring me a wild boar that you've killed with a reed of maize and I'll know how brave you are. We'll see what you can do with that old sword and that dagger with the crack in it! Now tell me what your scheme is.' Then mother and son sat down together in that secluded room and discussed Hambir's scheme for hours. When twilight neared, Rani Lachhmi said: 'Now get ready. If you delay any further, it'll be night.'

'I don't need to get ready,' said Hambir. 'I'll go as I am. Ma, will you please see if my horse has come?'

Rani Lachhmi left. Soon she returned with Hambir's horse. When he saw it, he laughed. 'Ma, now you'll see what I can do with this old sword, this cracked dagger and this nag of a horse.'

The queen blessed her son. 'May you be victorious,' she said.

Hambir, in everyday clothes, tucked his primitive sword into his belt and mounted the old and feeble horse. The twilight deepened. The sun set. The horse clopped slowly through the village paths and entered the forest.

It was pitch dark inside the dense jungle on the Aravalli mountains – one would not have been able to recognize a person from a distance of even two feet. Hambir let his aged horse go, wrapped himself in a black blanket and hid in the darkness. As if he were a shadow himself, he disappeared in this realm of shadows. Just as a tiger hunts for its prey, Hambir began to search silently for the dacoits on the banks of mountain streams, on the edges of the densest thickets and in the caverns on the sides of the mountains.

Days passed. When he felt thirsty he drank from the streams, and when hunger struck he ate fruits from the trees. He slept inside caves. In this great forest, where it was all a deep green darkness, whether it was day or night, and filled with the roars and growls of tigers and bears, Hambir searched on. The forest seemed endless.

One night, when there was no moon in the sky and it was impossible to walk through the jungle, Hambir climbed a huge sal tree and sat dejected on a branch, looking this way and that. *Will I ever find the bandits,* he wondered. *It's hopeless trying to move around tonight. I'll have to spend the night up here. Uff, just listen to those mosquitoes buzzing around the trees! And there go the tigers again, roaring! I have never heard so many mosquitoes buzzing and tigers roaring. In any case, I'm not going to set foot on the ground tonight. This part of the forest is less dense than the others, but there seem to be a lot of beasts here.* Hambir tied himself tightly to a thick branch of the tree and fell asleep.

He woke up in the dead of night. He could see an orange glow in a corner of the sky. Thinking that dawn was coming, he sat up, and then it struck him – if the sun were about to rise, why were all the birds silent? Had he made a mistake? He started looking all around. Soon he heard two men talking at the foot of the sal tree he was on. He could not make out what they were saying, but he distinctly heard the names Munja and Sujan Bahadur being mentioned.

Slowly and silently, Hambir climbed down to a lower branch of the tree, from where he could listen in on the conversation. The two men were clearly from the Bhil mountain tribe. 'Brother Badri, you still call him Munja, that's why he gets angry with you,' one was saying.

'Why shouldn't I call Munja by his name? Doesn't he know that I'm his uncle?'

'Brother, he doesn't recognize any uncles any more. From the day he defeated the Rajputs and that son of the Rana, he has been losing his head. Now he wants that we call him Rana and his son the prince.'

'Oh, drat that Rana and prince business. I'm going to always call them Munja and Bhunja.'

'So then, brother, why are you going now to watch the dances? It's the chief's daughter's wedding and he must be already fully drunk on mahua. If he spots you he'll cut your head off.'

'Do you think I'm a sacrificial buffalo that I'm going to go and put my head right on the chopping block? Come on, let's go have some fun at my grand-niece's wedding. You've already wasted half my night with your meaningless chatter.'

The men hurried away northwards. Hambir now understood that he was close to the dacoits' den. He could hear the faint sound of drums and cymbals in the distance. The reddish glow that he had noticed in one part of the sky was from the light of flaming torches at the ceremony. Hambir climbed down from the tree quickly and followed the two men.

Many days had passed since Sujan Bahadur had set out into the jungles. Unable to catch the bandits, he had returned to Kailur. There was no news of Hambir. Almost everyone had come to believe that he had been killed by Munja's men. And then a letter from Hambir arrived at the Maharana's court. It said that he had made Munja Bahadur the Rana of Mewar and had given him the throne. In return, the new Rana had awarded Hambir all rights to the fortress of Kailur and a hundred villages surrounding it. So it would be preferable, Hambir had written, that Ajaysingh peacefully leave the fortress, otherwise there would be war. No one should be in any doubt that Munja Bahadur himself would come with his full army and seize the fortress. Hambir had written this letter from the village of Ujala.

The letter was read out in court. 'The audacity of that boy!' said Sujansingh. 'Does he really believe that he can capture the throne of Mewar with a handful of bandits?'

'Can Hambir fall so low?' said Ajaysingh. 'I

cannot believe this. Does not the letter sound slightly suspicious?'

'It is very hard to believe it, but one cannot really say anything with any certainty,' said the chief minister. 'I think it is better to be prepared for battle. One can never tell with these boys nowadays.'

'Let us then inform all the chieftains of Mewar,' said Sujansingh.

'There is no need for that,' said Ajaysingh. 'This is not the Pathan Badshah coming that we have to call all our chieftains. People will mock us. Tell everyone to stay alert. It should not happen that the fortress is suddenly attacked by the dacoits again. Write back to Hambir that he should refrain from such a misadventure. Sujan, take some soldiers with you and chase those dacoits out of Ujala. And if you can, catch Hambir and bring him here.'

Sujansingh bowed and left the court. But he had faced Munja once and had learnt very well that this man was no ordinary bandit. He went to his bedroom and sent the royal physician to the Maharana to tell him that he was very unwell and needed to rest for a few days. Could not the army chief be sent instead for the battle?

'All right, let it be so,' said Ajaysingh.

That night, Ajaysingh met Rani Lachhmi and showed her Hambir's letter. The army chief was then called to the queen's private quarters. He left with a letter for Hambir and clear instructions: follow Hambir's advice and move with great caution.

Meanwhile, at Ujala village, like the lowly fox who thought it was king, Munja Bahadur sat all resplendent on his throne. On either side of him sat two new ministers, Gambhirmull and Chuamull, with quills stuck behind their ears. The rest of the court consisted of Hambir, a couple of fat landowners from the village and a few burly Bhils.

A poor peasant had been unable to pay his taxes and the king's men had brought him to the court in chains. 'Off with his head!' Munja ordered. At once Hambir whispered in his ear: 'If you do this, all your subjects will be angered. I suggest a small reward be given to the man.' So a gift of two gold coins was announced immediately and the peasant salaam-ed Munja several times and left. And he said to himself: 'Hambir is the real king. That man who pretends to be king is just a leader of some dacoits, he has no compassion or pity in his heart.'

The Maharana's army chief now arrived from Kailur and presented himself before Munja Bahadur. After some discussion, it was agreed that Ajaysingh would hand over the fortress of Kailur to Hambir and go into exile in the holy city of Kashi with his entire family. The Maharana's expenses would be paid from the treasury. Hambir would rule Kailur as Munja's representative. He would be paid all his expenses and a monthly salary of six thousand gold coins. He would also be awarded the right to collect taxes from the fort of Chittor.

Gambhirmull dictated the terms, Chuamull wrote out the agreement and presented it to his master. But the master was illiterate; so, quill in hand, he looked at Hambir.

'It may not be safe to sign such important documents with a quill,' said Hambir. 'It may be better if the king puts the seal of his handprints on it.'

Munja Bahadur smeared his palms with ink and put his handprints on the agreement. The army chief left with the document. Munja Bahadur had a good belly laugh. 'This is such fun!' he told Hambir. 'No battle, no bloodshed, no problems – just two handprints and the deed is done. How about sending a document with my handprints to the Badshah of Dilli and going and capturing the fort of Chittor?'

'Let us first take Mewar, and then we will push on to Dilli,' said Hambir. 'Perhaps the king can order some celebrations now? Let the Maharana's general too see what sort of splendid parties we can throw.'

'Friend, organize the revels the way you want,' said King Munja. 'But don't forget the drums and the mahua. Without these two it'll be boring.'

Hambir arranged for dozens and dozens of jugs of mahua and many drummers. Fountains of joy erupted in the king's palace at Ujala. Everyone came – Kairul's army chief, Gambhirmull, Chuamull, Hambir and the Bhil king's subjects from the villages all around. And with them came Rajput soldiers dressed as civilians in white.

The night was almost over and the villagers had all gone back home. The Bhil soldiers had finished off all the mahua and were now rolling around on the ground when, with a bloodstained jute bag in his hand, Hambir mounted his old feeble horse and departed Ujala. The army chief was ordered to burn down Munja's palace.

Many weeks ago it had been evening when Hambir had set off from the fortress of Kailur on his aged horse. It was evening again when he returned on the same horse with the crown of Mewar and the head of Munja. Ecstatic celebrations broke out in Kailur.

The Maharana dipped his finger in the fresh blood from the Bhil's severed head and put the royal tilak on Hambir's forehead. 'The rule of the Rajputs is that before one ascends the throne, he must perform a penance worthy of the tilak. This blood of our enemy brings your penance to an end. From today, the throne is yours, the crown is yours. But remember that though the crown of Mewar has been recovered, our land is still in the hands of the Pathan invaders.'

Then the Maharana called Sujansingh, gave him five weapons and a horse and told him: 'Leave Mewar and go south. Wherever you gain the power to do so, set up your own kingdom and rule it. Do not think that I do not love you, but I have realized that your exile will be good for both Mewar and you. If the Almighty wishes so, one day your descendants will rule a vast and united kingdom in the south. Go, and always keep in mind that you are a scion of the Dynasty of the Sun. May your deeds never bring disrepute or shame to the dynasty. Rely on yourself. Only then will you be able to attain greatness.'

Sujansingh rode south and eventually settled in the Deccan. His most glorious descendant was Chhatrapati Shivaji.

6

Hambir Wins His Throne

Hambir was no longer just Hambir – he was now Maharana Hambir of Mewar, Regent of Ekalinga. But that title was far more impressive than the actual size of his kingdom. All he had was the fortress of Kailur, some villages around it and two thousand Rajput soldiers. In reality, the Maharana of Mewar was merely a country squire.

Meanwhile, Maldev sat in Chittor and ruled all of Mewar on behalf of Muhammad Khilji, the Badshah of Dilli. The fortress of Kailur stood around twenty leagues from Chittor. On a clear day, one could see the fort of Chittor on the distant mountaintop, like a ship floating in an ocean high up in in the sky.

Hambir would often go up to the terrace of his fortress with Ma Lachhmi and gaze at the citadel, much like a pilgrim gazes at an idol of his god. He would watch the light of the morning sun slowly unveil the skyscape – beginning with the stone walls of the royal palace and the golden spire of the fort's great temple. 'Look, Ma,' Hambir would say. 'My ship has appeared.'

'The ship is there, and ready,' the queen would say. 'But if you stay asleep, what is yours will be owned by others.'

'No one in this world can keep my ship away from me,' Hambir would say.

On the day of Deepavali, Rani Lachhmi realized that Hambir had hardly been asleep. He had been quietly planning his moves to ascend his throne. In the evening, Hambir came to his mother and said: 'Ma, come with me to the terrace if you want to see all the lights.'

'You are all grown up and you still haven't got rid of that habit of joking with your mother?' said the queen with a smile. 'Where did you find Deepavali lights in these barren fields? Is this your Chittor, where every home is lit up?'

'Come with me and see,' said Hambir, and took his mother up to the terrace. It was the new-moon night of the month of Kartik and the sky was filled with stars, as if the gods were showering flowers down on earth. The queen, amazed, kept staring up at the sky.

'Isn't it a splendid sight, Ma?' said Hambir with a laugh. 'But that is the Deepavali of the gods – not yours, not mine. Now look at Kailur's Deepavali and tell me how it looks – come, look this way.'

The queen lowered her gaze and saw that all the hills and mountains around Kailur were lit up. In the villages, on the roads and fields – in every direction, hundreds of thousands of lamps shone and glowed and glittered. They were an enormous garland of stars, a huge web of light. Stunned, Rani Lachhmi looked up at her son's face and asked: 'Hambir, where did all these lights, all these people come from in this desolate Kailur?'

'All those lamps that you see on the mountains, they have been lit by the Bhils,' said Hambir. 'And all those in the plains, they are lit by the villagers.'

'But all these lamps, so much oil, did you get them from Chittor?' asked the queen.

'Not only from Chittor,' replied Hambir. 'I got potters to make the lamps and millers to grind the seeds for oil from all over Mewar. Look there – the torches have been lit in the potters' village. They will march out now. Listen to the drumbeats from where the performers live – now all the comedians and clowns will appear. Listen to the grand music from the merchants' quarters and the fireworks! Can you see, Ma, how beautifully the Brahmin girls have decorated the banks of the lake with their lamps?'

'How amazing!' said Rani Lachhmi. 'You've built a whole city! And all this time I thought you were just sleeping! Why did you never let me know that you had such intelligence and foresight?'

'Let all that be, Ma,' said Hambir. 'Now you have to choose a nice name for this city of mine. What do you think of "Lakshmipur"?'

'No, no,' said the queen. 'That sounds like a Bengali name. I'll look for a good name. And not only for a name, but also a bride for you who will be as auspicious as Lakshmi the Goddess of Prosperity. Please wait a few days.'

While the two were talking, an emissary from Maldev and a priest had arrived from Chittor with a marriage proposal for Hambir. The priest gave the queen a letter from Maldev and a coconut covered in silver foil. Rani Lachhmi read the letter. Maldev had written: 'My daughter is as beautiful as Goddess Lakshmi and as talented as her sister Saraswati, Goddess of Knowledge. Please accept her as your maid and sanctify our lineage. I may be serving at the pleasure of the Pathans, but I have not abandoned my Dharma.'

The queen looked at Hambir and said: 'See what a

nice coconut Maldev has sent us from Chittor. It'll be marvellous to use it in our Deepavali puja tonight.'

'Yes, that's a nice coconut and I have been eyeing it from the moment I saw it,' replied Hambir. 'Let's not give it to the gods. Give it to me.'

'All right,' laughed the queen. 'You can have it. After all, the king is also some sort of god. But you can't just take the coconut and go away. You'll also have to accept the daughter of the person who has written this letter and sent the coconut. Take the priest with you and write a proper and polite reply to the letter. Let me go and do my puja in the meantime.'

'Can you tell me what is going on?' Hambir asked the priest after Rani Lachhmi had left.

'Maharana, come, let us talk,' replied the priest. 'I will explain everything to you.'

Soon after, the emissaries returned to Chittor, having finalized the details of the wedding.

Preparations began in Kailur for the groom's journey to Chittor. But several elderly Rajput chieftains came to Rani Lachhmi and told her: 'Maharani-ji, please do not forget that in spite of whatever Maldev may be saying now, he is on the side of the enemy. It is not advisable at all to send the Maharana to Chittor without any protection.' So the queen ordered five hundred soldiers to accompany the groom and his party.

Hambir touched his mother's feet before he set off. The queen blessed him and said: 'My dear boy, along with Maldev's daughter, may the mother goddess of Chittor too welcome you and make you her own.' Hambir's horse seemed to almost grow wings as it galloped towards Chittor.

It was nearly evening when the groom's party arrived in front of the fort. The setting sun had lit up the whole western sky, as if a band of angels were holding a huge luminous umbrella over the Maharana's head.

But where was Maldev, whose daughter was set to be the queen of the great kingdom of Mewar? He was nowhere to be seen. The single guard at the gate of the fort touched his forehead to the ground to show his respect for Hambir. But there was no blowing of conches, as custom dictated, no joyous greetings and welcome from the family and friends of the bride. It seemed like Hambir was about to enter an abandoned city.

'Maharana, this seems very suspicious,' an aged minister murmured to Hambir. 'I do not like Maldev's conduct. I think it will not be safe to enter the fort.'

'Why should I be afraid to enter my own fort?' asked Hambir. 'Come on.'

As soon as he had spoken these words, Maldev emerged from a corner of the gate and said: 'Maharana, that is what I was hoping for too. You are returning to your own home, so what is the need for a grand welcome or song and dance?'

'Maldev, do you not know that it is the Rajput tradition that the groom has to first capture a fort made of flowers and only then can he enter his future father-in-law's home?' asked the minister. 'Why have your daughter's friends not organized that?'

'Sir, I am certainly the father of the bride,' replied Maldev. 'But where is my home? This is the Maharana's fort. He is entering his own home. How can my daughter's friends dare to put any obstacles to his entry here?'

'I see that all the hobnobbing with the Badshah has cured you of many superstitions,' said the minister with a smile. 'Come now, let us get the wedding ceremony done in the right manner. Rani Lachhmi has ordered that we must return to Kailur with the husband and the wife by night's end.'

When Hambir was led by Maldev into the great hall where his father and grandfather had sat in court, his heart went through a great storm of emotions that he himself could not describe. He thought he could see a row of valiant warriors in golden armour surrounding the empty throne like shadows. They held their swords aloft and were all looking at him, but none of them spoke a word.

The eyes of all the Rajputs who had come with Hambir were fixed on the throne. In the half light of that vast hall, it seemed as though the gold canopy over the chair would glitter for a few moments and then disappear into the darkness and shine again and obscure itself once more. Then, as Hambir's five hundred Rajputs were getting to their feet after paying their respects to the throne, Kamalkumari came in with her friends and put a garland of lotus flowers around Hambir's neck. The whole hall seemed suddenly lit up in all its glory.

It was as if the mother goddess of Chittor had been living all by herself, like a helpless widow in a corner of a derelict palace for so long, and now the prince of Chittor was holding her by the hand and reverently welcoming her back home. No one could recall how many years it had been since conches had been blown in holy joy in the fort. It had lain desolate for years, most of its rooms empty with heavy locks on their doors. Now, with the calls of the conches and the clanging of swords by the five hundred Rajputs, it seemed for a few moments that the fort was again filled with happy crowds, that its past splendour had returned.

Hambir returned to Kailur with his wife but came

back two years later and captured the fort of Chittor. Vanveer, Maldev's son, had been hoping that he would succeed Maldev. Now quite desperate, he sped to Muhammad Khilji, the Badshah of Dilli. He then advanced on Chittor with Khilji and his Pathan army.

The Badshah set up camp at the village of Singoli a few miles from the foot of the mountain on which the fort of Chittor stood. Hambir sent off Kamalkumari and their one-year-old son Kshetrasingh with Rani Lachhmi to the Kailur fortress and set off for battle.

The Rajputs fell on the Pathan army the way a tiger attacks a herd of deer. Muhammad Khilji did not return to Dilli. Hambir put him in chains and hauled him to Chittor fort. Vanveer too was captured. Hambir did not have him executed because he was, after all, Kamalkumari's brother, and took him to Kailur as a prisoner.

Hambir stayed on in Kailur and Muhammad Khilji was kept in Chittor under strict security. A month passed, then two, and then three, but Hambir showed no signs of returning to Chittor. Finally, one day, Rani Lachhmi asked him: 'Have you ceded Chittor to the Pathan Badshah? It doesn't behoove you to leave Chittor, where your throne is, and stay put in Kailur. Don't you want to be king and sit on the throne?'

'Ma, do you know what it takes to sit on the throne of Chittor?' replied Hambir. 'Snatching the crown back from the hands of Munja the bandit or capturing the fort from the Pathans is not enough to sit on the throne of Bappaditya. I cannot be king till I have found Ma Bhavani's falchion. No one knows where it is. Some say the Pathans took it when they looted Chittor, and some say it burned to ashes along with Rani Padmini in her Jauhar.'

'I don't believe either of these theories,' said Rani Lachhmi. 'Let people say what they want, I believe that Ma Bhavani's falchion is still in Chittor. The problem is, there is no one left in Chittor who can diligently look for it. But why blame the people? When the king of Chittor himself shows no initiative and makes no effort to retrieve it, why would ordinary people bother to find the falchion so that they can hand it over to the king?'

That night, Hambir touched his mother's feet and pledged that he would find Ma Bhavani's falchion before he did anything else.

The next day, the sky had clouded over at eventide and a slight drizzle had begun when Hambir and Kamalkumari, disguised as peasant villagers, reached Chittor fort. Kamalkumari showed the way, and Hambir, wrapped in a thick blanket and a huge turban covering half his face, cautiously followed her towards Chittor's great cremation ground. Black storm clouds from the east were now careening west above them. The branches of the big trees creaked and groaned in the high winds. Night fell. A downpour began. There was no one around and the skin froze when the gusts touched it. Amid the gale and the deluge, Kamalkumari arrived at the great cremation ground with Hambir. It was pitch dark, and all one could hear was the sound of what seemed like a waterfall.

Rani Kamal pointed in the direction of the rushing waters and told Hambir: 'Next to that cascade on the face of the mountain is a giant banyan tree. Right next to it is the entrance to a tunnel that goes into the underworld. It's through this tunnel that Rani Padmini went to consign herself to fire. At the end of the tunnel, in one of the caves, is the temple of Karuni Devi. I have heard that a python guards the mouth of that cave and that just above its head hangs Ma Bhavani's falchion. I have been to the entrance of the tunnel many times but never had the courage to go in.'

'Come with me to the tunnel,' said Hambir. 'You can stay under the banyan tree. I'll go in.'

From one corner of the cremation ground, a winding path led steeply downwards. Hambir and Kamalkumari, hand in hand, made their way down. In the dark they could not make out how far they had walked, but suddenly the path ended at a gushing stream. It emerged as a cascade bursting through the rocks. The stream was only knee-deep but was ice-cold.

Carrying Kamalkumari in his arms, Hambir began to wade across the stream towards the banyan tree. He could hear a harsh clanging noise that seemed to come from inside the mountain, as if someone were shaking a great metal gate. He grasped the root of the tree and climbed up to the bank of the stream. It was so silent and so dark here that it felt as if he had reached a place far away from earth.

Hambir set Kamalkumari down at the foot of the banyan tree and, with his arms outstretched to feel his way in the dark, entered the tunnel. Water streamed down the rock walls. There was no light, no sound. Hambir could see nothing before him, and nothing stirred behind him. He was alone in this indigo darkness.

His foot touched something and it rolled away. Hambir picked it up – it was a human skull. He was stepping on human bones that crumbled under his weight. He saw the root of a tree that had pierced the mountain wall. It felt like a strange reptile to the touch. Sometimes he thought he heard hissing sounds and sometimes the whispering of people. Mysterious flashes of light appeared and vanished in an instant.

In some places the walls seemed to recede from him and at places they seemed to move in so close that he could hardly breathe. Somewhere on his way, he thought he heard a congregation wailing. Sometimes his feet seemed to get stuck in mounds of ash. Far above him he could glimpse a sliver of sky, but he now found himself trapped in a circular cavern. Sheer walls rose all around him, and there appeared to be no way of escape. He groped around blindly in that dark underground space. His feet were sinking into a great heap of ash at the centre of the circle. There was no way to go forward, or up, or down.

Hambir did not know how long he had been standing there when he suddenly heard the sound of conches and bells from somewhere above the walls of rock. Then one wall split and parted along the crack, as if a door was opening. Through the gap, Hambir saw five bhairavis – priestesses of the occult – dressed in saffron, with strings of rudraksha beads wound around their necks. They were sitting around a huge iron cauldron set on a blazing fire. In the distance, the golden idol of Karuni Devi glimmered and twinkled in the flamelight. Hambir walked across the Karuni Devi temple to where the bhairavis were sitting.

'Who are you? What do you want?' screamed the women in an unnatural voice.

But Hambir felt no fear. 'I have come to take what is mine,' he said. 'I want the falchion that Ma Bhavani had given Bappa, which is here. My mother has sent me to take it where it belongs. I am Hambir, the Rana of Chittor.'

The bhairavis did not reply. They merely pointed at the red-hot cauldron. Hambir rushed forward, but as soon as he touched the cauldron . . . where did it go? And that raging fire and those mysterious priestesses? Hambir found himself standing before Rani Kamal with the falchion in his hand and some smoke slowly spiralling out of the mouth of the tunnel, like a python unwinding itself.

The day that Hambir sat on the throne with Ma Bhavani's falchion, celebrations broke out all over Rajasthan. And Muhammad Khilji, the Badshah of Dilli, offered Hambir a ransom of five million gold coins and pledged that he would never set sight on Chittor as long as he lived. He was then released.

Hambir let Vanveer go too, at Kamalkumari's request because it was she who had told him where he could find the falchion. He now renamed the fortress of Kailur Kamalmeer, after his wife.

And Rani Lachhmi, her son now truly the Maharana of Mewar, went back to her village of Ujala to spend the rest of her days in her childhood home nestled between the gurgling river and the fields of maize.

7

Chanda

Lakharana, grandson of Hambir and king of Mewar, had fought battles all his life, but was now old. His sword had lost its edge after decades of beheading enemies. It was not sharp enough to slice even a stalk of sugarcane now. But though his sabre may have become blunt and rusty, the Rana's words were still razor-sharp. No one could match the acerbity of his wit. In fact, with age his wit had only become more biting.

So one night, there he was, sitting all dressed up on a terrace of his palace, looking like a preening dove in white clothes, a long white scarf loosely wound round his neck and a huge sparkling-white turban on his grey head. Half of the marbled terrace high up on the mountain was lit up by the moon and the other lay in the dark shadow cast by the soaring walls of the fort.

His courtiers and acolytes were sitting around him, each with a clay tumbler of siddhi in hand.

The servants had brought in large bowls stacked with garlands and vessels filled with paan. The fragrance of roses and expensive perfumes wafted in the air. In a corner, women dancers were tying golden anklets around one another's legs. A music recital was about to start when an emissary of Ranamalla, the king of Marwar, arrived with a marriage proposal offering his daughter's hand to the crown prince of Chittor, and a coconut wrapped in silver foil. With the emissary was the prince himself, Lakharana's eldest son Chanda.

The emissary from Marwar was rather stout, his belly proceeding ahead of the rest of his body, which was peaked by a massive turban of eleven yards of cloth. It was only with great effort that Lakharana could stop himself from bursting into laughter at the sight of this spinning top in human form. But he could not resist the temptation to have some fun at his expense.

He took the silver foil-wrapped coconut from the envoy and said: 'This is nice! Has your king sent this for me to play with in my old age?'

The emissary should have replied that the coconut was no toy for an elderly greybeard and the marriage proposal was not for Lakharana but for his son, Prince

Chanda, but he stood tongue-tied at the Rana's joke. Everyone sitting around was smirking. The prince's face reddened in embarrassment.

The envoy was now in deep trouble. 'Maharana, it is a matter of great joy that you yourself have accepted our princess,' he stammered. 'Our king is not rich, how could he have dared to send a coconut with a marriage proposal to the Maharana? He hoped to have the prince as his son-in-law, and he cannot have imagined in his wildest dreams what you have said right now. If you give me permission, I shall immediately send word of the glad tidings to my king.'

Lakharana was at a loss for words for a moment. But as the emissary got up to leave, he caught him by the hand and said: 'Please wait. I was merely joking. Where is the prince?' But Chanda had already left. The Rana's men ran out to bring him back, but Chanda refused to return. He sent back the message: 'The princess whom the Maharana expressed a desire to wed, even if in jest, has the status of a mother for me now. I will never marry her.'

The Rana was stumped. How could the boy not understand a simple joke? He sent his courtiers and ministers again and again to Chanda to plead with him to change his mind, but Chanda stayed firm in his resolve. The Rana was now caught in his own trap. He had never thought his careless jest would turn into one of those big trees that magicians seem to conjure up from thin air. He did not mind marrying once more, but what really bothered him was that the joke was now on him and not on the emissary from Marwar.

Finally, when Chanda remained unmoved even after hours of entreaties to him, the old Rana twirled his grey moustache and yanked at his grey beard in fury and said: 'Chanda, you can stick to your vow. But I too vow that I shall give my throne to the son that will be born from this marriage of mine. He will be the Rana after me and you will have to live as just another chieftain under him.'

At once Chanda took a pledge in the name of Mahadev Ekalinga and said: 'It shall be so.' Everyone in the royal court sat in stunned silence. The envoy from Marwar returned with the message that the Maharana had accepted the marriage proposal.

Lakharana felt humiliated to have to dress up as a bridegroom and be laughed at by his own people, and he never forgave Chanda for his loss of dignity. Two years after the wedding, he placed his two-month-old baby Makul on the throne of Mewar and went off on a pilgrimage with just a blanket and a brass jug, never to return. No one knows where he went, and whether, if ever, he managed to escape the gigantic joke that life had played on him.

Since Makul was an infant, all the work that a king needed to do was done by Chanda. He was effectively the king without officially being the king. All of Mewar was full of praise for him. The people respected him and loved him as much as they feared him. And Makul's mother and her Marwari brothers found this intolerable.

Chanda did not say a word to anyone, but he knew that he would not be able to stay for long in this kingdom. Whom could he call his own any more in this great royal palace where he had grown up in the lap of his adoring mother and affectionate father? The queen had dismissed all the servants who had worked for the family for generations and replaced them with her own people from Marwar. Her brothers would barge into Chanda's private quarters whenever they wished to. From his bed to all his gold- and silver-plated furniture, everything was now Makul's property. The only thing he truly owned was his sword.

But Makul – as innocent as the bud of a flower, younger than him by twenty-five years, his little brother with the radiant smile who had not even learnt to walk or talk yet – was he not someone Chanda could call his own? Did not all of Chanda's worries and sorrows vanish in a trice when every day he carried the little one to the royal court and back and Makul hugged his neck with his tiny arms? Chanda had thought many a time of leaving Chittor, but those tender arms of his brother were both a chain that shackled him and a soothing salve for all his wounds. He was unable to break free and leave the child.

Year after year, Chanda silently suffered his inner pain and worked to make sure that Makul would grow up to be deserving of the throne of Mewar.

At the height of summer, when the court would be dismissed early, Chanda would take the boy out into the open fields to play polo – he on a stallion and Makul on a small pony. Under the blazing sky with no hint of shade anywhere, the horses of the two brothers would move as fast as streaks of lightning, chasing the ball. The wind would be like blasts from an inferno and the heat from the sun would turn the brothers' faces as red as blood.

On other days, when rain poured down from the massed clouds, Chanda would take Makul for a hunt beyond the villages in the faraway jungles and swamps – trudging through mud, getting drenched in the rain, swimming across rivers that had overflowed their banks.

On winter days they would have fun high up in the mountains, where the icy wind would tear into their chests like honed razors.

This was the way Makul grew up, getting stronger by the day. He did not live a life of luxury even though he was a prince. Chanda brought him up in the same way a common Rajput boy might have been, and not like someone who would be the absolute lord of Mewar one day. Chanda was preparing him right from childhood to be a fearless king in the face of whatever troubles and dangers and griefs that life would throw at him.

Makul's mother, however, did not like this. She wanted her son to grow up pink and plump, like a wax doll, resting comfortably in the cool breeze of a fan when it was hot, under an umbrella when it rained and tucked under warm quilts in the winter. So Makul, and sometimes Chanda too, would have to bear with the queen's rebukes. Makul, the child, would get angry at times at his mother's scoldings or even burst into tears, but would soon forget about it. But for Chanda the queen's words were like arrows that pierced his soul.

Sometimes he would tell some elderly chieftains who were his dearest friends: 'No more. I can stay here no more. Everyone says that I have put my brother under some spell and am going around being king. That he obeys all my wishes, so I am the real power and he is just a front – the king of Mewar only in name. Please relieve me of my duties now, let me go and stay in some other kingdom.'

'It is not time yet, Prince,' the aged chieftains would reply. 'Stay for a few more years. Let Makul be a bit more ready.'

Chanda wanted to hand over the responsibility of preparing Makul for the throne to some of the senior chiefs, but no one was willing to take it on. They would constantly say: 'Prince, we are ready to do anything in the service of the throne of Mewar, but in the end we are outsiders. You are his elder brother.' Chanda had no reply to that. Their father would never have asked Chanda to go through so much pain for Makul. But he was gone. Who else could take charge if Chanda, as the elder brother, did not train Makul for his duties as king?

Time passed. One night, in the month of Baisakh, after a seasonal storm had ceased, huge white clouds were moving westwards from the eastern corner of the dark sky, like ships with their tall sails at full mast voyaging across a black ocean. There was not a star to be seen and not a sound to be heard. Chanda had finished his day's work and was sitting in his room alone in the dark, gazing at the sky. It was very late now. His young wife, a Chauhan princess, was fast asleep in their bed. Everyone in the palace was in deep slumber. Only Chanda was awake.

A terrible sorrow deep inside his heart seemed to be twisting his ribs and trying to break them. Chandra could not understand what the sorrow was about, yet the pain was dreadful. All he could think of was – 'Let me call Makul and ask him to sit close to me.' But he was unable to either call out to him or even stand up. All he could do was to sit by himself in the dark in a sort of stupor. Both his mind and body seemed to have turned numb and seemed dead, only his eyes were using all the light that his soul could muster, to search hour after hour in the blackness of the rainy night for . . . But for what? Chanda himself did not know what it was that he was looking for.

The cold gusts of a gale stirred the trees, the houses, the water in the lakes and the sky itself before going on their way. Rain poured down in all directions. Lightning flashed and thunder rumbled before they too called it a night. Slowly, the clouds thinned, strips of silver appeared through the breaks in them, lightening the dark and the little dawn birds burst into song.

And then there it was – a solitary cloud brimming with water in the middle of the young blossoming light of morning. How beautifully serene it looked to Chanda – as if it were his mother! He could not take his eyes away from that cloud. All through the dark night his eyes had searched for this, for his dead mother, and now he had found what he had been looking for. The sorrow in his heart became quiet, much as the taut string of a bow when let go twangs and trembles down to a state of peace. He had watched the rain-drenched night clouds and had now seen the morning cloud born of his mother's tears. Looking out of his window at it, Chanda fell asleep.

It was now late morning. The bell rang, calling everyone to court. The queen had dressed Makul up and was waiting for Chanda to come and take the child to court when Makul's daai, the young king's governess and caregiver, arrived and said: 'The court will not sit today. Prince Chanda is unwell.'

The queen's father Ranamalla was in the room. 'Oh, so if Prince Chanda is not available, the court will conduct no business?' he snarled. 'Is Rana Makul a nobody?' The daai, who had also brought up Chanda, opened her mouth to reply, but the queen stopped her and said: 'Go away, I do not want to hear a word from you. My father will go to the court with Makul. Tell all the noblemen to be there.'

That day, instead of a scion of the Dynasty of the Sun, the pot-bellied Ranamalla sat on the throne of Mewar with his grandson Makul on his lap. The faces of all the chieftains turned red with shame and anger. And right at that time, Chanda woke up with a start and saw that the sun was in eclipse. It reminded him of a rotting dish of copper. He looked down and saw the aged daai sitting at his feet, weeping, her face covered in her hands.

After the court was dismissed, the Rajput chieftains came to meet Chanda, their faces as dark as the monsoon sky. Chanda addressed them with folded hands. 'The Maharani does not wish me to carry out royal duties any more,' he said. 'She told me this very clearly. Today, by her order, Ranamalla, the king of Marwar, has taken on the responsibility of looking after Makul. From now on, he will be in charge of the affairs of the state. I am free now. I bid you farewell and leave you to take care of Makul and the throne of Bappaditya. My horse is ready.'

All of them could sense the terrible torment that Chanda was going through. No one spoke. They bowed to him reverently and left.

Chanda then met with the daai secretly. 'Please make sure of Makul's well-being, make sure that he is safe,' he told her. 'My brother Raghudev is in Kailur. I'll meet him and then go on to meet the king of Mandu. Tell the Maharani that I will not be too far away, and if there is any danger to Mewar or trouble in the kingdom, she can always call me and I will come at once. My sword exists to fight Makul's enemies and my soul lives for Mewar. Daai-Ma, won't they let me see Makul once before I leave?'

The daai could only shake her head and weep. Chanda realized that there was no way that he could meet his younger brother. He did not say a word. He did not even change his clothes. Tying his sword to his waist, he mounted his horse and galloped away from the palace.

At high noon, when Makul began looking for his brother to go on their usual hunt, the queen told him: 'A tiger has eaten up your brother. He is gone forever.'

All day a tearful Makul kept searching for his brother in the palace but could not find him anywhere. At night, after everyone had gone to bed, he put his arms round his daai-ma's neck and said: 'When I grow up, I'm going to kill the tiger that killed my brother. I'll cut its head off with one stroke of my sword and bring it to you.'

'Ranasaheb,' said the daai. 'Tomorrow, I'll make a net with strong ropes to trap the tiger. We won't let it escape.'

Makul was silent for a while and then asked: 'Daai-Ma, what does the tiger look like? I've never seen it, so how will I know it?

'You'll know it,' said the daai. 'Or I'll show it to you. It has a pot belly, just like your grandfather, and also ugly whiskers and moustaches like him.'

Next morning, when the daai dressed Makul up and brought him to his grandfather in the court, Ranamalla twirled his grey moustache and glared at her. 'Daai, it will take time to make a trap for the tiger,' he said. 'So I will leave you to it. I am bringing a good daai from my land. She can do the work for the queen and you can go to the jungle and build your trap.'

The daai bowed low before Ranamalla and said: 'As you please, sir.' Then she turned to Makul and told him: 'Ranasaheb, you must get to know the tiger – pot belly, ugly whiskers and moustache, and big teeth, just like your old grandfather.' All the people in the court began to smirk. Makul took a look at Ranamalla and ran to the daai with fear in his eyes and hugged her.

The daai kissed him and said: 'Don't be afraid, dear boy. Never run away when you see a tiger. Use your sword, cut off its head.' Seeing that the people in the court were finding it difficult to contain their amusement, Ranamalla tried to take charge of the situation. With a hollow laugh, he patted the daai on the back, gave her a pair of gold bangles and told her: 'Very good, very good. I am so happy that you are giving him courage and making him strong enough to hunt tigers one day. I am increasing your salary by ten gold coins from today. Till Makul grows up, you will take care of him.'

Everyone in the court realized that if there was one person in the kingdom of Mewar who could outwit Ranamalla, it was the daai, and Makul had no better friend than her in the whole palace. The chieftains of Mewar, who, out of respect for the queen and fear of Ranamalla, had never spoken a word, could not help but praise the daai's courage silently. Ranamalla left the court hanging his head in embarrassment.

Chanda's younger brother Raghuvir was called Raghudev by all of Mewar because he was as handsome and brave as a god. He lived in a small stone house surrounded by gardens, far away from any city and the din of the kingdom, looking after the poor and needy. When he spoke, his words affected the souls of all who listened, high or low, like the most melodious music. He did not have a single enemy in the land. Even the queen, who treated Chanda hatefully, respected him like a guru and loved him like a brother.

And Makul could never forget the joy of listening to the stories that Raghudev told him, the picnics they had had with fruits plucked from his garden, climbing up to the nests of birds and feeding the little chicks there and learning to play the bamboo flute from shepherd boys in the shade of the trees.

Ever since Chanda had left, Makul had been crying every day, asking to visit Raghudev. The queen had even agreed to send him there for some days, but Ranamalla would keep raising some objection or the other. So the queen suggested that Raghudev could be invited to the palace, but her father would not let her do that either. Finally, one day, Ranamalla told her very clearly that no one could meet Raghudev without his permission. And then it was that the queen's eyes opened. She realized that she had no say any more in the kingdom – she and Makul would have to live like prisoners within the four stone walls of the palace.

Suddenly, news came that Raghudev had been travelling to the fort to meet Makul and had died on the way. Lamentation broke out across the land – everyone believed that Ranamalla had poisoned him. All across Mewar, people put up idols of the slain prince to worship and cursed their fake king and his gang as thieves, thugs and murderers.

The daai came to the queen and said: 'There is still time. If you want to save your son, send a message to Chanda and ask him to come. Otherwise, Makul too will one day meet Raghudev's end.'

But how could that message be reached to Chanda? Any person the queen entrusted to carry her letter would be a Ranamalla man. Ranamalla had packed the entire government of the kingdom with his own people. His spies lurked in the queen's private quarters, in the homes of the noblemen, in every village, school, temple and monastery. Information about anything anyone said or did quickly reached the pot-bellied Ranamalla, the king of dacoits and the monarch of thieves. Day and night his henchmen sat in watch at every gate and in every turret of the fort.

The queen was overcome with anger and sorrow. She could only see darkness all around her. She realized what a terrible mistake she had made by sending Chanda away. She fell at the daai's feet and wept. 'What will become of me?' she cried.

Tears welled up in the old daai's eyes. This was the woman whom the queen had once viciously tried to drive out. She calmed the queen down and said: 'I will arrange to have the message sent. But Rani-Ma, you must be very careful. No one must get to know what we talk about. If your father learns of this, we will be in grave danger. The whole kingdom is under his control. Even if he throttles Makul with his own hands, no one will utter a word. They are all too scared.'

After working out a plan with the queen, the daai went to the room where Ranamalla sat every evening, resting against a bolster as fat as himself, counting the numerous gold coins he had collected that day and putting them away in jute sacks. When he saw the daai coming, he quickly pawed the remaining coins into his lap and said: 'What – what, why this sudden visit at this odd hour?'

'Sir, just a little thing,' said the woman. 'If you are busy, I can come back later.'

Ranamalla feared the daai, just as a clerk fears the owner of the business he works for. Everyone in the kingdom was terrified of Ranamalla, but Ranamalla trembled at the thought of the daai. 'Not at all, not at all,' he blabbered. 'Let us attend to your thing first.'

'My lord, Makul-ji has a request,' said the daai. 'He wants to keep some pigeons, so I have come to you to present his case.'

'Makul-ji wants to keep some pigeons!' said Ranamalla, and had a big laugh. 'Very good, very good, these are nice hobbies – like teaching pigeons to fly and tending goats! I have no objections at all. I would be very relieved if he stopped riding horses or fighting with swords. Why should a prince be doing those things? Let him fly thousands and thousands of pigeons and live in peace, and . . .'

The daai interrupted him, '. . . And the prince's grandfather sits on the throne and stashes away sacks of gold?' she said.

'You are right, Daai,' said the rogue. 'I am very pleased with you. Keep Makul distracted with pigeons and kites. Just two more years . . . then we will see how anyone can take the throne away from me. Here, take this.' And, with great reluctance, he fished a coin out of a sack and offered it to the daai.

The daai folded her hands and said: 'May your gold coin stay with you. Makul-ji does not lack the money to buy some pigeons.'

'Of course,' said Ranamalla. 'Don't I know that? His mother has a lot of money. All right then, let her pay for a pair of pigeons. We are much behind in collecting the taxes from the subjects. I don't have a penny.' And he went back to counting his coins. The daai did a big salaam and left.

Some days later, in a corner of the fort's terrace, in the shadow of an overhanging stone balcony, two pigeons sat quietly in a cage of bamboo. Their throats swelled as the sun began to rise. Once in a while their white wings gently quivered at the joyful thought of Makul coming any time now to open the door of their cage and set them free into the radiant sky. The queen came with the daai and tied two little rolled-up letters under their wings and softly closed the door of their cage.

Dawn had not yet fully broken on earth and Prince Makul was fast asleep, his head on a soft pillow, his arm stretched out towards a window in the east with a piece of paper clutched in his fist, when the queen and the daai slipped into his room. The queen woke him up, placed him in the daai's lap and said: 'You're still asleep? It's getting late. When are you going to tie your letter to your brother round the pigeons' necks and send them off?'

Without saying a word, Makul jumped up and ran to the terrace, dragging the daai with him. 'But, Makul-ji,' asked the daai as she panted after him, 'you'd told me that you'd write a letter to your brother, where is that?'

The prince opened his palm and showed the daai a piece of paper covered with meaningless scribbles. The daai turned the paper over and over and then said: 'Very good. Now read out to me what you've written.'

Makul knew how letters were written, so he read out solemnly:

> Sir, I am your little brother. I weep because you are not with me. Please come and play with me. The two pigeons are carrying my letter. Please reply. When they have babies, I will give one of them to you. I am well.
>
> – Makul, your little brother
>
> PS: Mother and Daai-Ma weep for you all the time.

'Just as a letter should be,' said the daai, and rolled it up. 'So, tell me, which one of your brothers do you want to send the letter to?' This question flummoxed Makul. It was very difficult for him to choose between his two brothers – he loved both equally and wanted to ask both to come and play with him, but he had only one letter. His face darkened in confusion, but then the queen drew him close and said: 'You can do it this way. Send half the letter to your eldest brother and half to the other.' So Makul tore up his letter in two and handed the two pieces to the daai.

The pigeons spread their white wings and rose up into the sky with the two pieces of Makul's letter tied round their necks, and the two letters written by the queen and the daai hidden under their wings appealing to Chanda to come and protect Mewar against grave danger.

The two birds flew over the gold-crested clouds. The rays of the sun reddened the sky and fell on the two pairs of white wings like the wind on a ship's sails. When the pleas of Makul and his mother, helpless prisoners in the fort of Chittor, travelled through the dazzling morning, the heat-scorched afternoon, the overcast evening, past all the strange and wonderful play of light, and into the indigo-drenched night sky and reached Chanda in the fortress of Mandu, he forgot all the sorrows and insults he had suffered. He stood up and tied his sword, which had been lying in a corner of the room for a long time, to his waist.

For three days now, a massive storm had been blowing through Rajasthan. The sun, when it could be glimpsed a few times at dawn and dusk, was a deep scarlet. When Chanda had ridden out of Chittor, three hundred Bhils had come with him, with their bows and arrows. Now, at Chanda's command, they set off through the rain, storm and streaking lightning to return to Chittor.

At some distance from Chittor lay the town of Gosunda, named after the goddess Sundareshwari. A strong fortress stood on top of a hill, surrounded by a number of small houses. At the foot of the hill was a dense forest with many streams and rivulets running through it. Chanda and his men hid in this forest and waited. It had been agreed that the queen would use the excuse of offering puja to Sundareshwari to come here and meet Chanda on the night of Deepavali.

In the meantime, the Bhils loyal to Chanda spread the story all over Mewar that Ranamalla had killed Makul. This rumour enraged the people of every town and village in the kingdom. They began marching towards Chittor with their staves and swords and bows and arrows. They had vowed that if the story turned out to be true, they would not let Ranamalla live.

When Ranamalla heard the news, he trembled in fear. He did not know what to do. It was at this point that the daai came to him. 'My lord does not seem to be in a good mood,' she said. 'I have also heard something terrifying. Do you know that people from all over the land are coming here with their weapons to see Rana Makul?'

Trying hard to hide his fear, Ranamalla snapped at her, 'I am the king of Marwar and the ruler of all of Mewar,' he blustered. 'Do you think I will be scared of a few dozen sticks? Tell me if you have any other news.'

The daai lowered her voice and said: 'It seems that the men who are coming are a very tough crowd. You don't know the Rajputs of Mewar. I think you should find a solution while there is still time.'

Ranamalla pretended to be unafraid and asked: 'And what solution do you suggest?'

'Send Makul-ji to the villages on a hunting tour,' said the daai. 'Let the people see that their Rana is alive and happy and enjoying his sport. That will calm them down and they won't disturb you any more.'

Ranamalla mulled over her suggestion for some time, then said: 'It's not a bad idea. But they can't be allowed to roam around in the villages with their hunting weapons. How long does it take for a hunt to turn into a fight. Do you have any other ideas?'

'Then send off the queen and Makul-ji in a palanquin to offer puja at temples in the villages,' said the daai. 'The effect will be the same.'

This was an idea Ranamalla fully approved of. The angry villagers who had been marching on Chittor began going back to their homes, relieved.

The daai escorted the palanquin carrying the queen and Makul to the gate of the fort and came back. When she said her farewell, Makul asked her why she was not going with them. 'When I finish that net I had promised you for trapping the tiger, I'll come to you,' replied the daai.

The town of Gosunda was in a great festive mood on the day of Deepavali. The queen and the Rana were visiting the fortress, so the puja to Devi Sundareshwari had been planned on a grand scale. Lamps had been lit in every home, and every street shop had been decorated with colourful lanterns, paintings and mirrors. The shopkeepers were spraying passers-by with rose water. The boys of the town were lighting huge Roman candles that blew up fountains of fire on the streets. They threw firecrackers at the horsemen who had come with Makul, scaring the horses and watching the fun. From small children to the very old, all the people were enjoying themselves. Fireworks of every description were set off – sparklers, flares, rockets, fire wheels, bombs and bombettes and every other sort of fizzing, wheezing, flying and flaming things. It was great entertainment, and a lot of smoke too.

Today Makul's happiness was beyond all measure. He rode around the town on a black horse dressed in gold, looking at the lights of Deepavali. But the queen stood alone in the dark, on the terrace of the fortress. As the hours passed, she grew more and more anxious that Chanda might not come. He was supposed to meet her at Gosunda on Deepavali night, but where was he?

Finally, when the lights of the town were being put out, Makul returned to the fortress on his horse, but there was still no sign of Chanda. There was no time left now – the queen and Makul would have to return to Chittor that very night. She looked up at the dark sky and wept. Her tears dropped silently on her breast and wet her dress.

The bells of the temple of Devi Sundareshwari rang out to mark the hour of ten. The royal entourage was ready with the palanquin for the journey back to Chittor. Makul was calling for her to come, but the queen found herself unable to lift even a foot off the cold terrace floor. The bells had now fallen silent, but the air and the sky still seemed to be vibrating with their echoes. Suddenly, ten rockets soared up from the foot of the hill, like hissing serpents made of fire, and burst into a shower of flowers all across the black sky.

The radiance of the flaming blossoms seemed to turn the night into day. The people of the town rushed out of their homes on to streets and yards and roofs to gape and cheer at the fireworks, the likes of which they had never seen. The queen clutched Makul's hand and said: 'It's time. We must not delay any longer. Let's go.'

Makul wanted to stay on the terrace for some more time and watch the splendid fireworks, but the queen dragged him down and pushed him into the palanquin. The rockets, high above them, rained down flowers of red light and vanished into the blackness. Makul thrust his head out of the palanquin, eager to see the next blaze of rockets, but the sky remained dark and still.

After waiting for quite a while for the rockets to reappear, Makul fell asleep. The palanquin was moving slowly across a desolate field. The queen could hear no sound from anywhere other than the soft *khass-khass* the feet of the eight palanquin bearers made on the ground. She sat quietly, looking out into the blackness outside.

At one point she thought she heard a band of horsemen galloping at a far distance; at another point she saw a man with a spear standing silently by the pathway, but when the palanquin came close he melted into the dark. When she had seen the fireworks over Gosunda, the queen had known that Chanda had arrived, but she had been unable to spot him. Only the sounds and sights that lurked in the shadows told her that he was somewhere nearby.

It was the dead of night now and the palanquin was approaching Chittor. The queen could see the walls of the fort rising pitch black against the sky. The palanquin began to climb up the mountain towards the gates of the fort, but Chanda had still not appeared. There were no hoofbeats of horses to be heard, nor the clanging of swords. The queen's heart sank as the gates of the fort opened slowly, like the maw of a giant demon.

The palanquin entered the fort. The queen turned her head and looked back. A band of horsemen, holding their swords to their temples, had entered through the gate behind her. Their leader sat on a mighty black stallion. He was dressed in black from head to toe. The queen could see him only for an instant, but there was no way that she could not have recognized Chanda.

They had barely entered when cries of '*Jai Makul-ji ki jai! Jai Chanda-ji ki jai!*' rent the Chittor sky and hundreds of men of all ages who lived inside the fort came out of their homes with their swords unsheathed, surrounded the queen's palanquin and walked with it towards the royal palace.

Ranamalla's people had been strutting around all this while, as if they owned Chittor. But the moment they heard Chanda's name, they fled like rats to look for holes to hide in. None of them had the guts to inform Ranamalla about Chanda's arrival. And how would informing the scoundrel have helped him in any way? Drunk on siddhi that Deepavali night, he was snoring away in his cot.

The daai tied him tightly to the cot with thick ropes and climbed up to the terrace to watch the fun. All the guards that Ranamalla had, with all their swords and all their shields, could only flail around like creatures of straw. The battle was won as soon as it began.

Chanda broke the locks of Ranamalla's private palace and entered. The noise woke up Ranamalla, and when he opened his eyes he saw men standing around him with swords held high. He also realized that he was bound to his cot.

But, after all, he was the king of Marwar and had both courage and physical strength. The sight of the swords had instantly cleared his head of all the effects of the siddhi. He stood up, carrying the cot on his back. 'Untie me, and then let's see who wins and who loses,' he yelled at Chanda. 'You are a warrior and the son of a king. But I too am a king. Have you fallen so low that you will tie me up like a beast and kill me?'

Chanda stepped forward to untie Ranamalla, but the daai ran in and shouted: 'Get away, get away! Let him burn to death!'

A heap of gunpowder which the daai had hidden in a corner now exploded with a huge boom, and within moments the whole room was up in flames. No one knew when and how the daai had smuggled in a big stack of firecrackers here – small, sneaky firecrackers that went by the name of 'weasel', that treacherous little animal. And Ranamalla burnt to death like a weasel. He kept banging on the doors and yelling: 'Open the doors! Open the doors!' but no one came.

The ropes that the woman whom he had always treated like a slave tied him up with were now great flaming snakes that embraced and consumed him.

Ranamalla had dreamt of presiding over two kingdoms – Marwar and Mewar – but now even Marwar was brought under the rule of Mewar. His son Jodharao, having lost his father's throne, ran away with a platoon of soldiers in tow, far away from the kingdom to the other bank of the Luni river.

All the land on the other side of the Luni – the plains, the mountains, the lakes and the forests – was ruled by the great warrior-sanyasi Harwa Shankal. All of Rajasthan bowed before him, for his great feats in battle and his compassion. None dared to question any of his orders. He saved people in danger, wiped the tears of the sorrowful, provided shelter to the homeless. All his soldiers were sanyasi-warriors committed to crushing every oppressor and tyrant.

They had built their fort in mountain caverns deep inside the jungle. Buried under the earth were huge cauldrons filled with coins, which they gave away to people who came to them in distress. Their weapons were stored in massive underground chambers, to be used to help those in danger. This was the dominion of Harwa Shankal.

Jodharao swam across the Luni in the dead of night and appealed for shelter. He knew that even Chanda might not want to get into a fight with Harwa Shankal. Shankal welcomed Jodharao to his land. But his home was rather small, so the soldiers who had come with the prince had to sit on the ground under the trees. The sanyasi-king got a bit worried. All these men had come a long way and would be hungry. But how could he feed so many stomachs so late in the night? He called his people and asked them to arrange for meals for Jodharao's soldiers. But there was no food to be found anywhere other than some atta. Shankal had given everything away that day to the poor and needy, and to his guests.

All his men were looking at each other, stumped. Shankal said: 'But we do have to feed our guests. Let's see what we have.' In a corner of a room lay a sack of red spinach leaves which were meant to be crushed to extract a dye for the cloth the sanyasis wore. 'Come, let's cook these,' said Shankal.

The sanyasi who served as cook laughed. 'Lord, this is a great idea for serving our guests,' he said. 'After all, the mouths that will eat your food may hate it but will hardly dare to criticize your hospitality when they go back to their homes tomorrow morning. This is a great idea.'

'I will do the cooking tonight,' said the lord with a smile, 'Let us all eat together. Invite all our people, ask them to come.'

A fire was lit under a tree and the cooking began. The heady smell of the food spread through the forest, but all those who saw what was being cooked instantly lost their appetite, even though they had eaten nothing since morning except for a handful of chickpeas. But they could hardly refuse their lord's invitation to eat. When the food was ready, the dining area was laid out for the guests.

Harwa Shankal gave Jodharao and his men thick rotis made from atta and the leaf preparation, and when they – the guests – had had their fill, he sat down with all his people to eat. They called out many times to their sanyasi-cook to come and join them, but he had wrapped himself in a blanket and hidden quietly somewhere deep in the jungle.

When the meal was over, everyone praised the food heartily and got ready to go to bed. None of them had ever thought that leaves could be cooked to make such tasty food. Some of them were talking about having the leafy vegetable every day with rotis, when the cook reappeared. Hearing all these compliments, he felt extremely guilty and foolish. He had imagined that the people who ate those leaves would get poisoned and drop dead like flies. But now everyone had their tummies full and were happily going off to sleep and he was the only one suffering serious pangs of hunger on this chilly night.

A winter night is long, but it did end, though only after causing the cook much discomfort and pain. He woke up at dawn and headed for the forest with an axe to get some firewood for cooking. There was an elderly Marwari soldier washing his face in the water of a cascade that descended from the mountains. His beard had been white the night before, but now it was splotched all over with red.

The cook could not contain his glee. He ran back, laughing, to tell all his mates about this hilarious development. There he found that every soldier of Jodharao's who had a grey or white beard was stroking it and looking at the others in utter confusion. All their beards were now red. No one had figured that their beards had been stained with the colour from the red spinach leaves. They were going mad, wondering how their beards could have drops of blood on them.

Now the sanyasi-king appeared. But the saint's beard was still white as snow. 'Do not be afraid,' he said. 'The sun that you are waiting for to grant you happiness is rising. Look around and you will see that its glow already lights up your faces. Rest here for a few days, and then we shall work out how we can get your kingdom back.'

That day, the cook brought another sack of red spinach leaves to his lord and said: 'I have to cook and serve this today.' The sanyasi-king smiled. 'Your beard is still black,' he said. 'The red won't show. Let it get grey and I'll paint you with the red from these spinach leaves. Today, go and cook some vegetables that our guests will savour.'

This man was as good at cooking as he was at eating. And he was a storehouse of outrageous and absolutely untrue tales. Jodharao and his people thoroughly enjoyed their stay with him; they quite forgot that they were living in a jungle.

Harwa Shankal's demand reached Chanda – Jodharao should be reinstated on the throne of Marwar and all the issues resolved without any bloodshed. This was Shankal's command and he would brook no dissent. Chanda's sons, Munja and Kantha, were looking after Marwar. Chanda told them that if Harwa Shankal or his men came to Marwar with Jodharao, the throne had to be immediately handed over to them.

When he heard of Chanda's decision, Harwa Shankal himself set off for Mewar with Jodharao and his soldiers. Their plan was meet Chanda and then proceed to Marwar. This went off as had been agreed on. The party reached Mewar and then began its journey to Marwar with Chanda. They camped near the fortress of Mandore, the capital of what had been Jodharao's kingdom.

The problem was that Jodharao was still very young. While everyone was retiring to bed, an aged Marwari came to him and whispered in his ear: 'We have come back to our land, so why are we sitting around quietly? Come, let us capture that fortress tonight. Surely, taking your throne back with your own force makes much greater sense than having it given back to you by your enemies? What do you think about that?' Jodharao could only agree with this, and all the Marwari soldiers crept away towards Mandore.

Chanda and Harwa Shankal had not had an inkling

about this treachery. When they stepped out of their tents in the morning they saw a horseman riding fast towards them, his turban unwinding and his breast bloodstained. When the lad reined his horse in before Chanda, he recognized him as his son Kantha. Harwa Shankal got him off the horse and laid him down on the grass, but he only had a last gasp left before he passed.

As they were wondering who could have killed Kantha and what was going on, Jodharao came galloping up to Shankal and Chanda. 'My lords, I ask to be forgiven if I have committed any crime,' he said. 'I was unable to beg to get back the throne that my father had sat on. But I have taken it now. Not through begging from you but with my own army. The battle is over. I have captured everything that was always mine. Chanda-ji killed my father as if he were an animal. I pay that debt back by killing his sons in fair combat. It is just repayment. If I have done something wrong, please punish me.'

Harwa Shankal sat for a long time, his head in his hands. Then he said, very softly: 'Jodharao, you have committed a huge crime. Chanda never did anything wrong. You are just a boy, so I will not punish you. But I want you to take a pledge that you will never again bear arms against Mewar. And that point where Kantha lies dead, that will now be known as the boundary of Mewar. Beyond that, it is your kingdom.'

Chanda's sight was blurred by his tears. But he could still make out in the morning light the little buds of aonla gooseberry blooming like flowers of pure gold all across the field where his son Kantha's lifeless body had lain. He looked at Harwa Shankal and said: 'Let these aonla flowers be the blossoms of peace. However far these flowers bloom, it will be known as the kingdom of Mewar to everyone. Lord, my work is over. Let me be your companion and cross the Luni river and take shelter in your abode of peace.'

'It shall be so,' said the sanyasi-king.

8

Rana Kumbha

Lakharana's son Rana Makul had two uncles – Chacha and Mair. Their father was from the royal family but their mother had been a woodcutter's daughter. As a result, their social standing was lower than that of the Ranas. There was no way that either could ever sit on the throne of Mewar.

But the brothers too did not have any ambitions to the throne. Makul had given them a lot of land, and there would have been no problem at all if he had just let them sit in the court quietly and not paid any attention to them. But he liked to have a bit of fun at their expense. One day he made them both warlords, each at the head of seven hundred soldiers, and sent them off to do battle.

The only thing the two uncles had ever been interested in doing was to smoke opium and happily doze through their days. Now, suddenly, they were chieftains and would have to lead troops on the battlefield. Oh dear! What sort of dangers could be lying in wait for them? Would there be a steady and sufficient supply of opium and tobacco? There would be no milk with lip-smacking cream out there, no sweet rabri, none of those delicious sweetmeats they loved. Instead, they would possibly die in the cold in those open fields! Makul had ordered his uncles to take care of the trouble that the Bhils of Maderia had stirred up and was enjoying the plight of the two men.

Soon the uncles decided that as long as the handsome salary due to a chief with seven hundred soldiers under his command came in on time every month, they had no problem about keeping their nephew entertained.

But Makul's pranks started getting bigger and sharper. It became impossible even for two men, lying around with their eyes closed most of the day in a haze of opium smoke, to not begin to feel the sting of Makul's barbs. Yet they knew that without Makul's benevolence, they would probably not even be able to get a good meal. So they could only keep fuming in silence. Once in a while though, a stray comment did escape their lips, but this would only add to Makul's enjoyment.

In the end, one day, the two uncles told him right to his face that he was on the throne only because of a tasteless jest of his father's, which had deprived the valiant Chanda of kingship, and that he would lose it too as a result of his craving to amuse himself. But even these clear and heartfelt words failed to open Makul's eyes. He kept needling his uncles and having his laughs.

Scarlet flowers bloomed one night in a forest, so bright and lovely that when dawn broke, they seemed to set the forest on fire. Makul and his court had set up camp nearby. While walking about in the jungle in the morning, Makul pointed at the flowers and asked someone what the tree on which they were blooming was called. 'We don't know much about trees, Ranasaheb,' the man replied. So Makul turned to his uncles and said: 'Do you know the name of this tree?'

It was a simple question, but the two uncles decided that since their mother had been the daughter of a woodcutter, the Rana was snidely implying that only they would have knowledge of trees. They had tolerated many slurs, but this was an insult to their mother! No son could stand for it. The two men resigned from their jobs immediately and left the forest, their faces dark with grief. Heads bowed, they went away, making their way through the crowd of chieftains, courtiers and soldiers.

They turned their backs on all the opulent clothes, all the weapons and wealth, all the servants, horses and elephants that the Rana's money had provided them.

Some months before this, they had adopted a little orphan girl they had found by the wayside and were bringing her up with all their love. With her in their arms, they left Chittor for ever.

Only now did Makul realize how much he had tormented his uncles and how unfair he had been to them. He sent many of his men after them to convince them to return, but they would not. The Rana sat alone all day, repenting what he had done. He was haunted by the memory of the shocked faces of those two simple-hearted men who had never hurt anyone and who had been his dependants. In the evening he set off from his camp and walked deep into the forest. The chieftains could sense their Rana's state of mind – they did not follow him.

But as light faded from the sky and darkness spread across the forest floor, they decided that it could be unsafe to leave the Rana alone in the jungle, where the rebellious Bhils could be lurking. They had just entered the forest when they thought they heard the sound of feet running over dried leaves. Someone was fleeing. And then they saw Rana Makul lying at the foot of the tree that bore the scarlet flowers.

Blood seeped from two spear wounds on either side of his chest. The Rana had been offering his evening prayers with his rosary, and the chain of beads was still wrapped around the fingers of his right hand.

Makul had been a beloved king. Entire Mewar went into mourning. And soon everyone began saying that this must have been the work of the two uncles. Surely, it would have been impossible for the Maderia Bhil rebels to enter the jungle and kill him!

~

The fortress of Ratkot stood desolate on a hill near the village of Payi. Chacha and Mair had reached there with much difficulty, after having wandered through many hamlets. But now Rana Kumbha, Makul's able warrior-son, and Jodharao of Marwar had joined hands and their men began to search for the two brothers in every village in every district.

Payi was a small settlement a long way from Chittor. It had just a few households of potters, metalworkers and farmers, most of them quite poor. When Chacha and Mair arrived among them and appeared to restore some of its lost glory to the ruined fortress, the villagers were initially very happy. All of them were invited to the fortress on festival days, and they visited the brothers and enjoyed their hospitality. But soon the two began to run short of money. They stopped calling the people over. After some time no one in the village even spoke much about them any more.

But then rumours began to circulate about the two old men up there in the ruined castle. Some said they had a lot of money, which they had buried under the fortress. A few villagers claimed to have seen that at three every night, someone with a lantern climbed up the hill to the fortress. Another person said that the two chieftains used a secret tunnel leading out from under the fortress to travel to Dilli, and that sometimes the Nawab of Dilli too came over for some fun and frolic. Someone's brother had clearly heard the strains of sarangis being played and women singing when he was returning late one night from the market.

A blacksmith had once gone to the castle to repair a couple of rusted door jambs. He told them he had seen the old men drop crushed iron into a cauldron filled with fresh human blood set on a mighty fire and the cauldron had then overflowed with molten gold. Two black panthers constantly prowled around the fire, sniffing the ground, he added.

Soon everyone came to believe that the fortress of Ratkot was a den of terrible evil, where ghastly acts were carried out daily. No one went near it. They thought they could hear the fierce roars of tigers from there even in broad daylight, and after night fell the *jham-jham* of sacks filled with gold coins as they were carried down the hill by mysterious horsemen.

Every month or two, the two chieftains would come down to Payi, load a lame horse with the clothes, wheat and atta they bought from the market, and go back up to the fortress. But each time they did so, the whole village would be agog for a week with new rumours and gossip. They were paying the merchant who sold them the atta with gold coins, not ordinary money! How much did ten seers of ghee cost, after all? How was it that the day after they bought the ghee, the milkman's wife was seen to be wearing a new silver necklace? And what was up with that cloth merchant? Why would these two old men be buying so many sarees from him? That man must have struck some secret dark deal with them!

While all these matters were discussed threadbare

in every home in the village, up on the hill the two old men were bringing up the little orphan girl they had adopted with all the love their hearts could hold. The girl was their very life, and that derelict fortress was filled all day with the child's laughter and the songs she sang in a voice as sweet as the most melodious cuckoo.

The little vines she had planted had crept up the decrepit walls of the fortress. They bloomed at dawn and dusk and added fragrance to the lives of two old men who had had to leave the land of their forefathers. There were only three human souls in the castle and a mountain dog as fearsome as a tiger. He was their servant, watchman and guard. There was no way a stranger could ever enter the fortress.

Just as a hawk builds its nest on a mountain peak and lives with its chicks, the two white-haired men lived happily in their unbreachable castle with their lovely adopted daughter for a long time.

Then one day, the daughter of the village constable of Payi went missing. No one had a clue as to what had happened. She could have drowned in the river or been taken away by a tiger. But everyone decided that the two old chieftains must have noticed the girl's beauty and kidnapped her. The father, half mad with anxiety and suspicion, began to hover beneath the walls of the

Ratkot fortress all day and night. He was convinced that his daughter was being held captive there, as one morning he himself had seen a girl, her hair loose, on a steep mountain pathway next to the castle. She was at a great distance from him and he could not make out her features, but he was in no doubt that it was his daughter.

So the people of the village advised him to go and complain to Rana Kumbha. 'No one but Rana Kumbha can rescue your daughter from the clutches of these powerful and evil men,' they told him. The policeman strapped on his rusted sword, mounted his horse, which might have been older than him, and set off for Chittor.

He had no idea how many days and nights it would take him to reach Chittor, but he kept on, crazed with grief, pausing once in a while to wave his sword at the fortress of Ratkot and hurl abuses at it. Late afternoon, he met three soldiers on horseback coming his way. When the three heard about the kidnapping of his daughter, they said: 'Come with us, Constable Sahib. You don't need to go to the Rana for this. We will finish off those two old scoundrels and get your girl back.'

'You say this because you don't know these two men,' said the policeman. 'They live in a castle which is impregnable. If anyone can get in there it can only be Rana Kumbha. You have to climb up the side of the mountain to reach it. There are no roads there. Tigers roar all day long in the jungles around it. Even if you manage to get there, you won't be able to come back, that's the sort of terrible place the Ratkot fortress is, where these two vile demons reign.' And then he broke down in tears, overcome by thoughts about his missing daughter.

'Do not fear,' said the youngest of the three soldiers. 'We will reach there. Come with us.' The policeman was irritated by the young man's confidence. 'So you don't believe me?' he said. 'I tell you, there is no road or pathway up to that castle.'

The young soldier was none other than Rana Kumbha himself. He had been looking for years for Chacha and Mair to punish them for the unpardonable crime he believed they had committed. He smiled at the policeman's words and said: 'If no human being can reach the fortress, how could these two old men have taken your daughter up there? Of course there is a path to get there.'

This made the policeman even more angry. 'Listen, young man!' he said. 'If there was any way to get there, do you think I would not have used it and instead be here on the road to Chittor? I would have cut off the heads of those two devils and rescued . . .' He started to weep again. The three soldiers calmed him down and took him back to Payi.

It was late evening when Rana Kumbha, disguised as a common soldier, reached Payi with the policeman in tow. Black clouds had massed across the sky – a thunderstorm was on its way. At the village the Rana learnt that the two old men living in the fortress were his uncles, Chacha and Mair. Kumbha was enraged. 'Come, there is no time to waste,' he cried. 'We need to punish these two devils right now!' Seeing the Rana galloping towards the castle, the other two soldiers followed. But not the policeman. 'They are mad! Mad!' he muttered to himself, shaking his head. He then ran home and locked himself in.

A storm arrived with high winds and heavy rain. When lightning flashed, the fortress of Ratkot on top of the mountain appeared like a pitch-black wave that had risen into the sky and was holding still. *Chhap-chhap* went the hooves of the three horses on the wet earth. 'We'll leave the horses here and cover the rest of the distance by foot,' said the Rana. The three men tethered their mounts in the jungle and began climbing the mountain.

Up in the tumbledown castle, the two old men and the girl they had adopted from the roadside sat in the weak light of a lone lamp in the midst of a vast darkness, chatting. At the broken gate of the fortress sat Hinguliya, the hunter dog, his hair as pale as a lion's, his big paws resting on the stone that marked the threshold, his ears alert for the slightest sound of anyone approaching.

The moist breeze carried to Hinguliya the scent of a wild flower that bloomed in the night. And right after that came the faint crunch of feet walking over twigs. The dog got up, shook himself once and moved silently towards the jungle. A soft warmth was rising from the wet mountainside; a few fireflies seemed to be searching for something with their lanterns lit. The dog reached the path that led up to the fortress and waited quietly by its side. These footsteps belonged to strangers. Hinguliya waited, silent and watchful, his eyes glowing like embers in the dark.

But the men who were coming up the mountain were no less alert – the expert hunter and warrior Rana Kumbha, his attendant, and Jodharao of Marwar. They did not mistake the two little flaming orbs behind the bushes for fireflies. They recognized them as the eyes of a fierce beast. The Rana's dagger flew through the air and pierced Hinguliya exactly where his loyal heart was beating.

The hunting knife had found its prey, the only creature that could have guarded the fortress, the only friend and defender the two old men and the innocent girl had ever had. Lion-hearted Hinguliya uttered one last cry. It pierced the darkness and was carried by the wind towards the fortress as a long wail. Perhaps he was trying to shout 'Beware!' And then he was silent. The storm wind blew.

For a moment, the Rana thought that he had killed a lion right at the entrance of the castle and was delighted. His companions too were happy. 'This is a very good omen, Rana!' they said. But then, when they came closer and saw that it was a dog and not a lion, they walked on at a much slower pace. None of them were feeling too eager any more about their mission.

Inside the castle, in that dark hall, the flame of the lone lamp around which the three people were gathered was now dying. Chacha was telling a story. His brother sat on a frayed rug and dozed, but the girl was listening avidly.

'The two of us were little children then,' Chacha was saying. 'I had learnt to walk but Mair was still being carried around in our mother's arms. Ma was going to Chittor, holding my hand, with Mair clutched to her breast. All the villagers were saying – "You are the daughter of a woodcutter, do you think Rana Kshetrasingh even remembers that he had married you? As if you're going to get anything at Chittor!" But Ma shook her head and we set off from our home. Our little home was next to a green meadow and a huge tamarind tree. I was feeling very sad and kept looking back at our home as I walked. But Ma never looked back – she walked with her eyes pointed straight ahead at the line where the earth met the sky.

'When the day was over, we would spend the night on the wayside somewhere or under a tree or even in an open field. When dawn broke, Ma would begin walking again. Sometimes, on an afternoon, we would reach a village and we would eat whatever alms the good people gave us. On other days we would get no alms and we didn't eat. That is the way Ma walked to Chittor – the abandoned queen of the Rana of Mewar, a woman who had lived by gathering wood from the forest.

'None of us knows how long we spent on the road. The rains came and went as we trudged on, drenched to the bone. Winter came. At night, the lawless winds blowing over the bare fields seemed to be pouring ice on us. Ma would wrap us up in a ragged blanket and stay up all night, weeping. Our abandoned Ma – the queen! On some days I would say, "Ma, let's go back home." Ma would say, "Just a bit more, and we'll be home."

'When I gazed ahead, all I could see was the chilly blue waves of a shadowy mountain. But Ma would keep walking towards that blue haze, and sometimes tears would pour from her eyes. Then one day – and I don't know how many days we had been walking and how far we had travelled, the sky went wet – just like today. The wind blew and lightning flashed. The mountain turned black in the shadow of the clouds and seemed to be moving closer to us. Ma was sleeping on the wayside; I woke her up and said, "Ma, look! So many big houses on the top of the mountain!"

'Ma opened her eyes and said, "That's our home!" Then she pulled me to her breast and hung a gold necklace round my neck and said, "Show this to the Rana, he will welcome you to your home."'

Chacha's eyes had filled with tears. 'And then?' asked the girl. 'What happened then?'

Chacha did not reply and the three sat in silence. After a long time, Chacha said: 'And then? He was the king of kings, and he welcomed my ill-fated mother into his home.'

'And what happened to you two?' asked the girl.

Chacha spoke softly and slowly. 'We went to meet the Rana,' he said. 'The two of us spent many years there, alone and together in happiness and sorrow. The king had such a huge palace – how could we ever find our mother there? We lived alone and wept for Ma –'

'Didn't you find your mother in the Rana's room?' asked the girl anxiously.

Chacha shook his head. 'No,' he said. 'How could we ever know where Ma was taken? Many years later, when both of us were old, one morning, when we were going to the court, we saw a child standing all alone on the wayside, crying, just like Ma, wanting to go home. We had found our mother whom we had lost such a long time ago. We placed her on our lap and we got on our big horses and came to this mountain.'

'But the Rana didn't come to snatch his woodcutter-queen back?'

'As if the Rana could ever find her!' both Chacha and Mair said together. 'We've hidden our mother away so cleverly in such a place that the Rana will never know!'

The girl was now very sleepy. She put her head in Chacha's lap and said: 'Will you take me one day to meet your mother?' Chacha ran his fingers gently through her hair and said: 'When you grow up a bit more, we will all tiptoe our way to that secret chamber where Ma has lit a lamp and is waiting for us.'

The girl looked at the door of the hall drowsily and asked: 'And Hinguliya too?' Chacha's brother Mair, now quite under the spell of the opium he had been smoking, nodded his head and said: 'Yes of course, we'll take him with us too.' By and by, all of them – the two who were telling the stories and the one who had been listening – fell asleep. Only the light of the lamp stayed awake in the darkness, its little flame the colour of gold that had been scrubbed with a touchstone.

None of them knew when the storm ceased and when Rana Kumbha, his sword unsheathed, entered the hall. There was a sudden crash of thunder and they woke up with a start to see three swords glittering over their heads.

'Get up,' said Rana Kumbha.

The two old men stood up, holding the girl by her hands. 'You murdered the Rana, you stole a Rajput girl,' said Kumbha. 'You will have to face your punishment now.'

'The Rana?' asked Chacha, confused.

'Makul-ji?' whispered Mair.

'Yes,' said Kumbha, 'and this is your punishment.' Two swords came down on two heads. The girl cried 'Ma!' and fell to the floor, unconscious. A sudden storm wind from an unknown direction blew out the lamp.

Kumbha believed that he had rendered justice to his father, who had been murdered by these two men. All of Rajasthan came to believe this too, except for the two dead men, who never got to know why they had been punished by the Rana. And the girl did not know either why she was then taken to the village constable's home and left there, and why in the morning all the villagers walked around her and told one another: 'This is not she, this is not our girl!'

She never knew why, after much discussion and argument, none of which she could understand, the villagers took her out of the village and left her on the edge of a barren field and returned to their homes. She never knew why no one answered as she kept crying out through the night for her two fathers and for Hinguliya; why the fortress of Ratkot had disappeared in the darkness, and why, however long she walked and searched, she could never find her way back.

Having avenged his father's death, Kumbha now sat on the throne of Chittor. His wife Mira was beautiful, as were the songs she sang. She was the daughter of Rana Ratiya. Rana Kumbha had been enchanted by her beauty and her singing and had married her. However, there was a problem. The queen performed every duty that was expected of a good wife, but her heart lay at the feet of the idol of the God with the Flute, carved from black granite, in the temple of Ranchhodji, one of the many names of Lord Krishna.

The Rana was unhappy about this. He was himself a poet and wrote songs. He wanted Mira to sing them at the royal temple. But that did not happen. Mira was the god's handmaiden; she sat all day in the temple of Ranchhodji with the other devotees and sang: 'Says Mira, you cannot reach Nandalala without love in your heart.'

It became a matter of great embarrassment for the Rana that the queen of Chittor was out there singing in public, strumming her ektara, a lowly single-stringed lute made from a gourd and a stick of bamboo. 'Bar all the common people from the temple,' he ordered.

Overnight, huge curtains were hung all around the temple. No one could see Mira any longer. But she could still be heard, and people came from all over the land to hear the sweet melody of her songs. Just as a deer is entranced by the tune of a flute, so were the crowds listening to Mira singing in silent devotion with all their heart and soul and in utter delight. When told to disperse, they would not. When ordered to go home, they did not. They ignored every command that was issued.

One moonlit night, Mira, looking like a celestial creature in her gold and diamonds, was singing and dancing before her god on the marble platform in front of the temple. The Rana was playing the veena and the crowds were listening from outside the barriers. All of a sudden a diamond necklace dropped from the sky, like a garland of stars, and hung itself round Mira's neck. Startled, the Rana stopped playing. Mira took the priceless necklace off her neck and put it around the neck of the idol of Ranchhodji. She did not sing any more that night.

No one knew who had sent the necklace, but many a story spread across the land. Some said the Badshah of Dilli had presented it to Mira; some said the donor must have been a very wealthy man who had now detached himself from worldly affairs. There were other theories, but everyone was happy that Mira had given it to Ranchhodji rather than to the Rana. All the devotees of the god went around praising Mira.

This upset the Rana. He ordered that the devotees could visit the temple but Mira must stay locked up inside the palace. Having said this, he rode off to do battle with Mahmud Shah.

Mira's songs stopped. And all of Chittor became despondent. The devout wept at the temple and Mira wept inside the prison of her palace. Unable to see her Nandalala, she grew sickly, like a flower cruelly plucked from the wild and brought to the city.

The king won the battle and returned to Chittor amid much pomp. He threw Mahmud Shah, along with his crown, in a dungeon. All the masons and sculptors and builders of the kingdom got busy constructing a tall stone tower to celebrate the Rana's victory. But he could not win Mira's heart.

'Rana, I am Nandalala's maid,' she said. 'Please don't keep me locked up in my room. I can hear Nandalala calling – "Mira, come to me." Let me go, Rana. I'll beg on the streets and go to Vrindavan with Nandalala.'

But this made the Rana even more angry. 'You are the daughter of Rana Ratiya who is just a minor chieftain,' he said. 'You don't deserve the throne of Chittor! Go wherever you want to, I'll get a new queen.' Mira, queen of Chittor and maid of Nandalala, left the palace with her ektara to walk the streets as a mendicant. And the Rana set off to find a new queen.

The prince of Mandore was soon to marry the daughter of the Rathore chief of Jhalawar. On the night of the wedding, even as the groom was on his way to the venue amidst much pageantry, Rana Kumbha seized the bride from the ceremonial hall and brought her to Chittor.

This was not only a Maharana, but the great Maharana Kumbha who had snatched the bride. So no one in Rajasthan dared to say a word about the crime he had committed. But when Mira, living in Vrindavan, heard from the prince of Mandore that Kumbha had dealt a death blow to the love of two young people for each other, she could not sit still. She set off for Chittor with the Jhalawar princess's groom.

News reached the Rana that Mira was on her way to his palace, and why. He ordered the princess to be locked up under tight security in the garden of Jhalowan. He then wrote to Mira that he, the king of Chittor, would be happy if his queen were to return to him.

Along with his letter, he sent the key to the garden where the princess was imprisoned. If Mira wished, he said, she could open the gates to the garden and meet her. But if the prince of Mandore tried to enter the garden, he would meet his death. Because no man other than the Rana would be allowed to enter the private quarters of the woman the Rana had chosen as his new wife. The prince could enter only after leaving his head at the gates.

It was twilight, and only a single star glimmered in the sky. Only one room in the stone palace in the garden of Jhalowan was lit up. The lamps in that room were like the fire of love that burnt in the Jhalawar princess's heart for the prince of Mandore. Mira received the Rana's letter as darkness set in. She read it and realized that there was no hope. She wrote back a single line: 'If you have not loved and felt no love, you will never find love.'

She then handed the key to the garden to the prince of Mandore and left Chittor. The prince unlocked the gates and headed towards the light that burned in that one window in the palace, to meet his beloved for the last time.

Years ago, at the fortress of Ratkot, Rana Kumbha had blown out the lamp of love that lit the lives of two old men and a young, innocent girl. On this night too, with another stroke of his sword, he doused the lamp that the princess of Jhalawar had lit inside his own heart.

As Kumbha sat in his court the next morning, a builder came to him with folded hands and said: 'The Maharana's Tower of Victory is ready. What would be its name? It needs to be carved into the stone at the base of the tower.'

Rana Kumbha thought for a while and said: 'Call it Kumbhashyam, Kumbha the Krishna.'

9

Sangramsingh

Rana Kumbha had fought a lot of wars, conquered many lands and displayed unmatched valour, but there was no battle that could compare with the one he fought in Jhunjhunu. The celebrations that followed the victory were also memorable – the singing and dancing, the fireworks, the lights. For a full month, the nights in Chittor were as bright as the days. But then something strange began to happen.

Every morning from the day after he returned from that battle, when he arrived at his court, Rana Kumbha would twirl his sword thrice above his head and mutter some incantation in Farsi or Arabic that no one understood. Only after this would he sit on his throne. And this peculiar ritual did not stop after a few days. It became part of his everyday routine in court. The Rana grew old, but the sword-twirling and chanting continued.

Everyone was baffled by this behaviour, but no one dared to find out why the Rana did what he did. Once the Rana's eldest son Raimull had stood up in court and asked for the meaning of what his father was muttering and why he twirled his sword three times over his head. And the king had replied: 'Leave Chittor within twelve hours. A son does not need to know the reason for what his father does or does not do.' The ritual continued and the order was never taken back.

Raimull went into exile. His two brothers remained in Chittor. The youngest one was Surajmull, and the middle one was a man who was never referred to by his real name by the people of Rajasthan. Even today, he is known simply as Ghatirao or Hatyaro – the murderer. This Ghatirao killed his father by poisoning his food and took the throne. The people of Chittor, enraged by this terrible crime, decided that murder was the best medicine to cure a murderer, and began plotting to get Raimull back.

The throne at Dilli was then occupied by the Pathan Sultan Bahlul Khan Lodhi. Ghatirao was planning to get his daughter married to the Sultan and fully secure his own position as the king of Chittor. At this time the Rajput chieftains located Raimull in a distant land. Ghatirao tried to keep them on his side with generous offers of more land and money, but he could not win anyone over. How could any Rajput support a man who had killed his own father and wanted to send his daughter off to be the begum of a Pathan?

Seeing that his situation was grim, Ghatirao sped in secret to Dilli and finalized the marriage of his daughter with the Sultan. But as he was riding back to Chittor alone on his horse, hoping that no one had noticed his absence and the kingship was still his, he was struck dead by lightning. Raimull captured the throne.

When Sultan Bahlul arrived in Chittor to marry the princess, he found that Raimull was sitting on a mountain-top like a tiger waiting for its prey, with fifty-two thousand horsemen in front of him and eleven thousand foot soldiers beside him. The Sultan, who had come in his best finery for the wedding, quickly wrapped his silk lungi around his waist, abandoned his silver-threaded shawls and ran right back to where he had come from – Dilli.

Raimull ruled Chittor for many years. He was aided by his three sons – Sanga, Prithviraj and Jaimull – and his brother Surajmull.

One day he was resting in the marble chamber that

rose from the centre of the great Bhim lake. The Rana was now quite old and his sons grown up. There was peace and prosperity for all in the kingdom of Mewar, from the nobleman to the commoner. It was noontime at the peak of summer, and venturing outdoors was like walking into a fire. The Rana's sons were lazing in their uncle Surajmull's garden retreat, amusing themselves with the diversions of the wealthy – games of chess and cards and idle chatter. Servants waving huge fans made from the giant and dense khus grass, sprayed with rose water, tried to keep the house comfortable for them.

But it was blazing outside. It was so hot that cracks had appeared in the mountains and every wall was radiating heat. So, though the three princes did everything to stay cool indoors, they could not for too long. And before they knew it the conversation had progressed from casual prattle to serious arguments, from minor quibbles to disputes about who among them was the best warrior and how many districts each had captured. They finally came to the question of which of the three was best qualified for the throne of Chittor. Who, they argued, was rightfully the man who could keep all his subjects content and would also be good for the kingdom as a whole?

Prithviraj, the Rana's middle son, was as handsome

as he was brave. Sanga, the eldest son, did not look like a prince at all. He was small built and soft-spoken, with deep and solemn eyes. Jaimull, the youngest, was burly as a bull and unpolished in his words and demeanour. Their uncle Surajmull was hardly very handsome, but he was hardly ugly either, and his eyes and nose resembled the Rana's.

The three brothers got into a huge spat over the throne of Chittor. 'If the choice is left to our subjects, be sure that Rajputs will choose me as king,' said Prithviraj. 'I don't care for all that,' said Jaimull. 'Look at these arms of mine. Might is right.'

Sanga, the eldest, smiled and said: 'I am sure Ma Bhavani has already decided whom she should give the throne to. If you don't believe that, we can go to the temple of Charani Devi, the goddess of soothsayers, and ask her whose destiny she sees the throne in.'

Surajmull was very angry by now. 'What is all this talk?' he said. 'If my brother gets to know of this, he won't spare anyone. Maybe I too will be thrown out of the land along with you three. Why all these squabbles about the throne? Do you think this is just another idle game of chess where you take this queen or checkmate that king and feel proud about it? Here, apply some rose water to your heads, cool down and let all these things be.'

But the heat outside had now taken hold of the princes' minds; how could they cool down? All three rose to their feet and said: 'Uncle, we don't need the cool breeze right now. Come, let us go to Charani Devi and ask the soothsayer to do her calculations and tell us who will get the throne.'

Surajmull was an intelligent man. He saw that if he went with the princes his brother would be furious; and if he did not he would anger the three sons of the Rana, one of whom was a great warrior and another a dangerous thug. So he decided to go along with them. 'It looks like the kingdom will come to me in the end,' he said. 'Either my brother will throw all three of you out tomorrow, or you'll kill one another in the next few days. Only I will be left to bear the burden of ruling the state.'

'That's why we are taking you with us,' replied Prithviraj. 'We need to know what the lines on your forehead foretell too.'

Surajmull tapped his own forehead and then the foreheads of the three brothers. 'We don't need a soothsayer to read the lines,' he said. 'These sounds are good enough. All these heads are hollow and our destinies too are quite blank.'

Naharamungra was five leagues from Udaipur. Here

rose a mountain known as Tiger Peak. The temple of Charani Devi, who could reveal the future to her devotees, was hidden in a dark cave high up the mountain. A yogini who had achieved supernatural powers through her penances looked after the devi. When the princes reached the temple, having ridden their horses hard through the wild heat, the yogini had gone out to gather materials for her evening puja. The cave was empty. All one could see were the three glittering crystal eyes of Charani Devi set in black rock and a huge stone platform. In the evening light that poured on it, the altar appeared to be drenched in blood.

When he saw that the yogini was not there, Surajmull said: 'Didn't I tell you that all our destinies are blank? There's no one in the temple. Let's offer our respects to the goddess and go back home.' But Prithviraj shook his head. 'No,' he said. 'We will sit here and leave only after the evening puja is over and we have had our palms and foreheads read.'

There was a tiger skin on the floor on one side, and on the other the yogini's bamboo-and-rope cot with a ragged rug on it. Prithviraj quickly went and sat on the cot and Jaimull joined him. The cot uttered a loud squeak under Jaimull's weight and then fell silent. Sanga sat on the tiger skin on the floor. Surajmull rested one knee on the skin and the other on the stone floor, which was as hot as fire.

The sun had set and the darkness inside the cave had deepened when the yogini entered with a lamp in her hand and saw the four men who were waiting for her. Sanga rose, held his folded hands to his forehead and sat down again. Surajmull did not get up, but he bent down and touched his forehead to the ground in reverence. Prithviraj stood up and bowed his head slightly, raising his folded hands a bit towards his forehead and then dropping them. Jaimull neither got up nor folded his hands. Sitting on the cot, he said: 'Mata-ji, please do your calculations and tell us who among us is destined to sit on the throne of Chittor.'

The yogini did not reply. She only rubbed her brow and began wiping her face with a corner of her saffron attire. 'This is a matter of great importance,' said Prithviraj. 'Please give it a lot of thought and do your calculations thoroughly and give us the answer.'

'Let her first offer her puja to Charani Devi,' said Sanga, 'and then she can address our question.'

'Yes, that is better,' said the yogini and sat down for the puja. She moved the lamp in a circle before the idol, rang the bell, did her puja and then stuck some marigolds she had offered the goddess in the turbans of the four men. 'Let me tell all of you princes a very old story,' she said. 'Many years ago, one day in the city of Ujjain, the great king Vikramaditya had finished his work in the royal court and had retired to his private quarters. As he was about to sit down to a meal, the goddesses Lakshmi and Saraswati appeared before him, arguing fiercely with each other. The king rose to his feet at once and said: "I am your humble servant, please tell me what brings you here."

'The goddesses blessed him and said: "Dear son Vikramaditya, you are a king. Please use your judgement and tell us who between the two of us is the greater goddess." Devi Saraswati's voice rang out like a sharp note from the veena she carried in her arms: "Is she greater, or am I?" Devi Lakshmi seemed to speak at a pitch even higher when she asked: "Who is greater, me or that one there?"

'The king found himself caught in a bind. If he judged one of them to be the greater goddess, he would enrage the other. But as he stood before the two, scratching his head, his young queen said: "Devis, please allow the king to eat something. He has been sitting in court all day, taking decisions and passing judgements. His mind is tired, so how will he be able to reach the correct verdict right now? Please give him a night to think this case through and he will announce his judgement in the court tomorrow morning."

"'That is a very good suggestion," said the king. "This is a knotty issue, it will be nice if I get some time to mull over it." The goddesses agreed and vanished. Vikramaditya sat down to his meal and asked his queen: "You have got rid of the goddesses for the day. But have you thought about the verdict that I will have to pass tomorrow?"

'The queen grimaced and said: "What do I know about solving a case? You have nine jewels in your court – the navaratna – pandit, poet, statesman, engineer and whatnot. Go and ask them."

'The king scratched his head some more and returned to his court. All the nine jewels were present – Dhanvantari, Kshapanaka, Amarsimha, Shanku, Vetalbhatta, Kalidasa, Ghatakarpar, Varahamihira and Vararuchi. But even after discussing the issue till the dead of night, none of these great scholars could offer a solution to the king's problem.

'If the king declared that Devi Saraswati was greater, Lakshmi, Goddess of Wealth, would be furious. Vikramaditya could lose his kingdom and the nine jewels of his court would certainly lose their fat monthly salaries. But if he gave his verdict in favour of Lakshmi,

Devi Saraswati, Goddess of Knowledge, would strike back – and that would mean the end of all education and learning. Kalidasa would no longer be able to write another epic poem; there would be no more of the pioneering work that Dhanvantari, the greatest physician on earth, was doing in the field of medicine, or of the discoveries that Varahamihira was making in astronomy. How would the king himself have all the intelligence required to run his kingdom, go through its finances and pass fair judgements to settle disputes?

'Vikramaditya was now deeply worried. He dismissed the court and took to his bed. The queen noticed that the king was unable to sleep and was restlessly tossing and turning, as if he had contracted that dreaded disease where the patient feels that he is lying on a bed of thorns that are pricking him all over . . .'

Prithviraj interrupted the yogini here and said: 'All of us know that story. The goddesses were offered two thrones to sit on, one made of gold and the other of silver. When one chose to sit on the gold throne and the other on the silver one, the judgement was reached automatically about which goddess was the greater one. Let the story be. Tell us now who among us is going to be the king of Chittor.'

The yogini looked at the four men and smiled. 'You

too have made the verdict easy and obvious by choosing where you would sit,' she said. 'Sanga sits on the tiger skin, the seat apt for great warriors. He will be king. Surajmull sits on the ground, close to Sanga – this means that he will have control over land and be close to the throne in a position of power. Prithviraj, Jaimull, you sit on a ragged rug on a sanyasin's cot. There is nothing more to your destiny than lying on some rags and dreaming of the throne.' Having said that, she vanished into the darkness of the cave temple, leaving the four princes to glare at each other like tigers.

It was Surajmull who broke the silence. 'So, now what?' he asked.

'So now it will be decided who the throne should go to right here,' said Prithviraj. He unsheathed his sword and advanced on Sanga. Sanga tried to run out of the cave, but the sword struck one of his eyes. A brother had shed a brother's blood before the altar of Charani Devi. To save his life, Sanga jumped on his horse and rode away into the darkness. The three others too mounted their horses. Surajmull sped in one direction, Prithviraj and Jaimull in another, each one determined to ambush the others. The night soon shrouded them all.

Almost a full night's journey away from the temple of Charani Devi stood the earthen farmhouse of the Rathore chieftain Bida. The farmhouse was shaped like the dome of a castle and guarded by high walls. Dawn was about to break but the rays of the sun had not yet streaked the overcast sky. Bida's pet peacock sat quietly under the huge tamarind tree in the courtyard, its head nestled under its wings. The two bulls that pulled Bida's plough dozed in peace close by.

There was not a sound to be heard anywhere, other than from near the gate, where a young Rajput stood with the chieftain's horse. Once in a while the horse shook its head and the old iron rings in its mouth that fastened its reins would jingle *ting-ting-jhin-jhin*.

Bida had planned to travel to a faraway village that morning to offer a puja. He was about to leave when he heard hoofbeats from afar, out there in the darkness. Someone was galloping hard towards his home. Soon Prince Sanga, drenched in blood, was shouting 'Help me!' and pounding his fists on the gate. Bida hurried to open it. One of Sanga's eyes was slashed and the rest of his body too was bloodied. When he recognized the prince, Bida asked: 'What is this? Who did this to you, sir?'

Sanga explained everything to him in brief, that his life was in grave danger. Surajmull and Prithviraj were lying unconscious somewhere on the road after having fought with each other, but Jaimull was still chasing him, intent on murder. Bida gave Sanga his own horse and said: 'Prince, please go inside and rest. You can take this fresh horse and travel to another village in a while.'

Sanga knew that Jaimull would be rushing down over the fields like a summer storm and wanted to flee immediately, but Bida, ever-faithful to the king of Mewar, would not let him go until he had fed and looked after the prince. Seeing Sanga hesitate, Bida said: 'Please do not fear. Leave through the back door only after you have rested fully. Till then, Jaimull will not be able to cross the threshold of this home. I shall keep him at bay.'

And that was what happened. Sanga rode out east on his fresh horse as soon as the sun had risen. By the time Jaimull, after three hours of fighting Bida, entered his home, Sanga was long gone – a tiny black spot beyond the vast fields, soon swallowed up by the dark forest. Only the exhausted and wounded horse that he had ridden up to Bida's house stood in the courtyard, peacefully chewing some dry grass.

In dismay, Jaimull struck his own forehead with his hand, red with the blood of the loyal and valiant Rajput warrior he had killed. He stared at Bida's lifeless body for some time. Then he skulked away, his head bowed, his shoulders drooping.

It was morning now and some peasants from a nameless village who were walking to their fields found the two princes – Surajmull and Prithviraj – lying on the roadside in pools of blood. They carried them back to their meagre homes. By now the Maharana had sent his men, with horses and palanquins, to bring the princes back. But they could find only two – Surajmull and Prithviraj. No one knew where the other two had gone.

Under the care of the queens, Prithviraj slowly recovered. Surajmull took more time since his wounds were more severe.

The Maharana had been told of what had transpired between the four princes. He called Prithviraj to his court. 'You are the one who is to blame for what has happened,' he said. 'Sanga is fully innocent. We have no information about where he is or whether he is even alive. If he is still alive, he is hiding because he fears that you will kill him. Do not assume that I am going to allow you to live in comfort in Chittor and that when I am gone you will just walk up to the throne and sit on it. Take as many horses and weapons as you want and get out of Chittor right now. If you really want to fight, go and defeat the enemies of our kingdom if you can, not fight your elder brother. If you can do that, I will know how deserving you are. Go.'

After ordering his son away, the Maharana called Surajmull. 'I will not punish you, since you tried to save Sanga,' he said. 'But you will now go and live with our cousin Sarangdev. Do not even think of coming back to Chittor.'

Surajmull went into exile and Prithviraj set off for his battles. He knew that the Maharana would forgive him only if he crushed the enemies of Chittor and proved his valour.

The king might have been angry with him but the people of Chittor did truly love Prithviraj, so he had support on his quest. A few men joined him as he left Chittor, and then, slowly, he gathered a band that was loyal to him and whose job was to go and fight wherever they could or wanted to. But after travelling across many lands and fighting many battles, Prithviraj began running out of money. In fact, one day he found that he did not have enough money to even buy food for his army. The only way out was to conquer a small kingdom or two and rule over them. He sent his ring, inset with many gems, to a jeweller called Ujha from Gadwar and asked him for some money in exchange. Ujha was the man whom Prithviraj had bought the ring from a long time ago, and at a very high price.

The moment he saw the ring, Ujha rushed with the money to the inn where Prithviraj was then staying in, disguised as a common citizen. 'What is this, Prince?' he asked. 'If you needed money, you could have just sent me a letter. Why would you want to pawn this ring and lose all the respect you have?'

Prithviraj took Ujha aside and explained his situation to him. 'I have nothing left in this world other than this ring,' he said. 'Anyway, I would have had to sell this ring one day just to survive. Look at all these people who fight by my side. I cannot let them go around underfed and despairing.'

Tears welled up in Ujha's eyes. 'Prince, take this money,' he said. 'I don't need the ring. I am your subject. I have eaten the salt of the Maharana all my life.' Prithviraj hugged him and said: 'Bhai, you have saved my life today. But what about the future?' Ujha lowered his voice and said: 'Defeat the Meena king and occupy his land. You will get rid of an enemy of your kingdom and also gain much respect.'

Prithviraj, heavily disguised, quickly went with all his men and enrolled in the Meena king's army. The Meenas of Rajasthan were a wild and fearsome race that excelled in looting and plunder. Their king, who called himself Meenarai, ruled over all of Gadwar and was defiant of even the Maharana. His den was in a village called Nadala. Prithviraj conferred with five of his most trusted men and made a plan to get rid of him.

The festival of Aheria was celebrated with great enthusiasm all over Rajasthan. On that day, both lords and servants came together to make merry with hunts and picnics, and Meenarai was no exception. But as he was drinking and having fun with his chieftains, Prithviraj and his soldiers attacked. They killed the king and burnt down the village of Nadala. The Meenas who survived ran off into the jungles. Prithviraj paid off his debt to Ujha by appointing him governor of Gadwar. He set off on more conquests, but now with a well-provisioned army.

Meanwhile, Jaimull, after much wandering, had reached the town of Bednore. Rai Surtan Singh, the king of Toda, had lost his kingdom to the Pathans and was at the time living in Bednore with his beautiful daughter Tarabai, under the protection of the Maharana. Tarabai was as intelligent, talented and proud a girl as she was beautiful. Many princes had expressed their desire to marry her, but Tarabai was firm that she would only accept the man who got her father's throne back from the Pathans as her husband.

Jaimull learnt all this in Bednore. One day he saw

Tarabai riding her horse to a hunt, armed with her bow and arrows. She looked like Devi Durga come down to earth in human form. Jaimull sent a matchmaker to Surtan Singh with a letter pledging that he would get the kingdom of Toda back for him. Surtan Singh was very pleased and invited Jaimull to stay at his home.

Days passed and then months, but Jaimull showed no signs of going to do battle with the Pathans. In fact, he was quietly plotting to murder Surtan Singh, take Tarabai prisoner and run away with her. One night, dressed in black and his face too painted black, he crept, sword in hand, towards the part of the palace where Surtan Singh's and his daughter's bedrooms lay.

He did not get very far unnoticed. He was spotted by the guards at the door to the king's private quarters. But Jaimull was a desperate brute; the guards could not stop him. He reached Tarabai's bedroom, caught her by the arm and tried to drag her out. However, Tarabai was no ordinary woman. She flung him away and leapt on him like a tigress. In a moment her dagger had put paid to all of Jaimull's evil intent. Surtan Singh came running and with one stroke of his sword sent the liar's head rolling on the floor.

Jaimull was the Maharana's son, and Surtan Singh, though a king, was living under the protection of the

Maharana. When news of Jaimull's death reached Chittor, everyone thought this would be the end of Surtan. But when the Maharana learnt the details of what had happened, he said to the messengers: 'Jaimull not only betrayed the trust of a king whom I have vowed to protect, he was also a liar, a cheat and a pig-headed fool. How can a father tolerate an attack on his daughter's honour? Surtan has given Jaimull the punishment that he deserved. It is good that such a worthless son is gone. I have no regrets. Please go and tell Surtan Singh that from today the kingdom of Bednore is his.'

When Prithviraj heard what his younger brother had done, he was overcome with rage and shame. He left immediately for Bednore. And when he met Tarabai, it was like a miraculous meeting of equals – one as good-looking as the other, each as brave as the other. For both of them it was love at first sight. But marriage was not possible till Tarabai's vow had been fulfilled.

Prithviraj swore on his sword that he would recover the kingdom of Toda from the Pathans. He left in disguise the same day for Ajmer. With him were the five men who had helped him bring down Meenarai, and Surtan followed at a distance with a huge army of Rajputs.

It was the month of Ashwin and the time of Muharram. The great bazaar square in the city of Toda was jam-packed with people and teemed with banners and replicas of the tomb of Husain the martyr. The people were armed with staves and spears and deadly brass knuckles, swords and shields, and were re-enacting the tragic battle of Karbala. The Sultan himself was watching the goings-on in the streets from the terrace of the Jama Masjid. Six fakirs carrying quite a big replica of the mausoleum and wailing loudly about Hasan and Husain stopped right below where the Sultan stood.

The Sultan leaned over the parapet to look at them. But that was the last thing he ever saw. An arrow shot through the air, pierced his chest and flew away with his life towards the sky. The Sultan fell back dead, and immediately the Rajput army attacked the city. The Rajputs of Toda quickly formed a protective shield around Prithviraj and Tarabai and fought the Sultan's soldiers. While the battle raged, all the Sultan's courtiers ran for their lives with their wives and their chicken coops. By morning Prithviraj had captured Toda.

News of the valour of Prithviraj and Tarabai reached the Maharana and it melted his heart. Jaimull was dead and no one knew where Sanga was – only Prithviraj remained, a son to be truly proud of. The Maharana oversaw the wedding of Prithviraj and Tarabai and gave them the fortress of Kamalmeer to stay in. This was the fortress on the border of Mewar, where Queen Lachhmi had lived with her little son Hambir.

For many years the fortress had lain desolate. Now, after many generations of Ranas had passed, Prithviraj and Tarabai filled up the empty rooms with laughter and song. It was a joyous time for all, father and son and husband and wife were now united. But then, one day, as Prithviraj sat in his father's court and the business of the day was almost done and the Maharana was about to leave, an envoy from Malwa arrived and demanded that the king meet him at once.

There had been a time when even an envoy from the Badshah of Dilli had to wait fifteen days before the Maharana of Chittor decided to find the time to meet him. But today the ambassador from Malwa barged into the court arrogantly and approached the king. And he did not stop at that. He sat down close to the Maharana and spoke to him as if they were equals. Prithviraj was amazed at the audacity of the man.

When the envoy had left after wasting everyone's time with useless chatter, Prithviraj asked his father the reason why he had treated the man with so much respect and concern. The Maharana patted Prithviraj on the back and said: 'You must understand that I am an old man now. I am like that toothless lion whom even a donkey dreams of kicking. You brothers were busy fighting one another, so for the last few years I have had to keep the peace all around by any means possible and be polite to our enemies to make sure that our land and all the assets that our people own stay safe.'

Prithviraj did not say anything, but he recognized the sadness at the core of his father's heart. He left the court, his head bowed in shame. He called up his loyal soldiers, reached Malwa and declared war on it.

The two armies had set up camp at two ends of a vast battlefield. The night before the battle was to begin, the king of Malwa was enjoying a lavish dance performance in his tent, reclining on some silk bolsters on his velvet carpet, when Prithviraj entered, collared him, dragged him to his own tent and locked him up. The performance had ended abruptly, the instant the light died out from the chandeliers that Prithviraj had casually destroyed. The singers and dancers were left gaping at the prince's daring and courage.

The commander of the Malwa king's army was hurriedly getting his forces ready when he received a letter sent by Prithviraj. It was a note written by the

Malwa king himself. 'I am being taken to Chittor as a prisoner,' it read. 'Do not even think of rescuing me. If any such attempt is made, I will be instantly killed. Stop your preparations for battle and come and meet me at once.'

This was after all the order of his king; the commander asked his army to retreat and went with his head hanging to meet Prithviraj in his tent. Prithviraj reassured him and said: 'Please do not fear for your king's life. I am taking him to Chittor and we will keep him in all comfort. We will return him hale and hearty. You will even get that supercilious envoy of yours back. The Maharana is not interested in keeping either your king or his envoy as prisoner. He has only commanded me to get the obeisance that Chittor deserves from Malwa. This is why it is necessary that your king visits Chittor. But if you try to snatch him in Chittor or on the way there, you will only recover his headless body. The head will be lying next to the low stool below the throne where the Maharana of Chittor rests his feet.'

The court was in session with the Maharana present when Prithviraj arrived with his prisoner, the king of Malwa. Everyone was astonished. And then one of Prithviraj's men brought in the envoy and said: 'Now why don't you learn from your king how to speak to the

Maharana?' The emissary stood there, trembling in fear, his body drenched in cold sweat.

The Maharana then took control of matters. He welcomed the king of Malwa and asked him to sit beside him. After they had enjoyed Chittor's hospitality for some days, the king and his envoy were allowed to leave and return to Malwa.

Soon after this, the Maharana's cousin Sarangdev and Surajmull, who had been staying with him, turned rebellious. Prithviraj was then far away at Kamalmeer. The Maharana sent a fleet horseman to inform him of what was happening and set off for battle. Surajmull had captured four districts of Mewar – Sadri, Batera, Nayi and Nimach – and had arrived on the far bank of the river Gaviri, very close to Chittor, with a huge army.

War began, and the Maharana's army was soon forced to retreat. It was evening and the Maharana sat in his tent, weakened by the twenty-two wounds he carried on his body. Surajmull's army now controlled the near bank of the river too. There seemed to be no way that the rebel force could be pushed back. Then Prithviraj appeared with one thousand Rajput soldiers.

The battle had been called off for the day. Both sides were now resting in their tents; torches and earthen vessels that carried fire blazed in every corner of the battlefield. Surajmull had fought all day and been injured many times. A barber had cleaned up his wounds and put poultices and bandages on them; he was now getting ready to sleep.

All of a sudden, Prithviraj entered and Surajmull leaped up from his bed so fast that the bandage tied around his chest split and blood began to spurt out of his wounds again. Prithviraj quickly laid his uncle down on his bed and said: 'Please do not fear. I've come only to find out how you are.'

Surajmull smiled a little and replied: 'Your sudden arrival made me a bit nervous. But I am delighted to see you after such a long time. Have you met the Maharana?'

Prithviraj laughed. 'I was in Kamalmeer when I heard the news about you and rushed here at once,' he said. 'No, I haven't met Father yet.'

A maidservant came in with dinner on a golden dish. 'Can't you see that we have an important visitor?' said Surajmull. 'Run along now and get us another plate of dinner.' The embarrassed maid stayed silent, looking hither and thither. 'Ah well,' said Surajmull. 'It seems that Sarangdev has sent only one dinner here. Let uncle and nephew eat from the same dish then.' As soon as he said this, Prithviraj picked up a sweetmeat and started to munch on it.

The enmity of the daytime disappeared in the shared sumptuous meal and idle joking and chatter that made both men laugh a lot. As he was leaving, Prithviraj told his uncle: 'Let our old fight be suspended for tonight. We will finish it tomorrow morning, what do you say?' Surajmull laughed. 'Agreed,' he said. 'Let us have a good night's sleep. But I will be ready tomorrow at the crack of dawn.'

The next day, Prithviraj defeated the rebel forces and Surajmull ran away with Sarangdev. But Prithviraj relentlessly pursued them, capturing district after district that the rebels had seized. The two went into hiding in the dense jungle of Nimach with their families. They took shelter in the secure and solid sheds they were able to build with the hard wood and branches from the mighty trees that towered all around them.

One afternoon, Surajmull was wandering in the jungle, chatting with his sons. There was no one else around other than a pair of blue pigeons cooing idly somewhere behind dense bushes. And then, like a tiger moving in total silence to pick the best instant to swoop down on its prey, Prithviraj jumped over the fence of the house that Surajmull had settled in and caught him. They wrestled with each other. Prithviraj had pinned his uncle down when Sarangdev stepped between them, pulled them apart and tried to calm Prithviraj down.

'What are you doing?' he shouted. 'Can't you see the state your uncle is in? He is old and weak – just one slap from you will send him flying. Let the poor man go!'

But Surajmull did not like Sarangdev's unasked-for intervention. 'That may be true, Sarangdev, that a slap from my nephew will finish me off,' he said. 'But it is also the truth that if that slap came from one of you, this weak body will only become stronger and will strike ten blows right on your nose. Step back. If an uncle and a nephew have to fight, they will do so on their own terms. If they want to make peace, it is up to them to decide. Do you understand?'

His uncle's grit surprised Prithviraj. Sarangdev glared at the two of them and left. Surajmull sheathed his sword and spoke to Prithviraj. 'The fight is between you and me,' he said. 'If I die at your hands I will have no regret or sorrow. Both my sons have turned out to be quite capable. If they find nothing better to do, they will join the Maharana's army. They will never draw arms against you. But if you die at my hands it will not be my shame and torment alone. Have you ever thought of what will happen to Chittor if my brother passes and you are not there? I will not fight you. If you wish to, kill me. But I will not allow you to take me with you as a prisoner.'

Prithviraj realized that Surajmull's soul was one with Chittor's. He threw his sword away and touched his feet. Surajmull hugged his nephew and said: 'I suppose that the prophecy has turned out to be a little bit true today. I am sitting very close to the throne of your heart. All that I wish for now is that I can lay my head down on a piece of ground in the land where I was born and take my last breath.'

Prithviraj sat down by his uncle, just like in the old days, and asked: 'Uncle, what were you doing before I came here?'

Surajmull laughed. 'I was just passing my time, narrating the history of Rajasthan to my sons,' he said.

Prithviraj was surprised. 'Surely you knew that I would come looking for you?' he said. 'But you were still sitting here chatting with no guards or soldiers to protect you?'

'You closed both my options, to fight or to run away,' said Surajmull with a smile. 'So why not spend some time with my children?'

'Why not come with me to my father and ask him to give you a place to rest your head on in Chittor?' asked Prithviraj.

Surajmull was silent for a while. Then he said: 'I could have done that some time back. But after the rebellion it makes better sense to find a place away from Chittor to rest my head. Maybe then I'll be able enjoy a few days with both my body and head intact.'

'That may be so,' said Prithviraj. 'But what about the fact that if I return to the Maharana without a head, I will have to keep my head bowed in what will be seen as failure? I may even lose my head.'

Surajmull lowered his voice. 'If Sarangdev's head helps you, you can take it,' he told Prithviraj. 'With his head will come his kingdom. With my head you will get nothing other than this torn turban. You will receive more acclaim with the other head.'

Prithviraj got ready, but Sarangdev was nowhere to be found. Prithviraj now started getting suspicious. 'You are not trying to trick me, are you?' he asked his uncle.

After some thought, Surajmull said: 'Come with me. If you can't get the big head, take the small one.' A little deeper in the forest stood the ruins of a temple. 'At one time, human sacrifice used to be carried out here,' said Surajmull. 'That stopped many years ago. The goddess has not received the fresh head of a human as an offering in ages. Sarangdev asked me to come here today to do a puja. Do you have the courage to go in my place?'

'Oh yes,' said Prithviraj. He unwound his turban and

tied Surajmull tightly to the trunk of a tree and entered the temple.

It did not take long. Prithviraj returned with the fresh head of Sarangdev, untied his uncle, recalled his soldiers and set off for Chittor as the victorious hero. Surajmull's army had taken control of several districts of Mewar – Nayi, Batera, Nimach – turning the hopes and joys of the people there to dust. Now he had to trudge back through these areas with Prithviraj, his head bowed in defeat. Only a small district called Sadri remained. And he wondered how long even that would be left to him.

Then one day, near a village temple, he saw a fierce dog trying to hunt a young goat. The father goat rushed in, rammed the dog with its head, sent it running and vanished inside the temple with its kid. The dog came back and stood outside the temple, barking, but did not have the courage to enter.

Surajmull decided that this was a safe place to stay in – this temple would be his home and his castle. He brought in architects and artisans from Sadri, built a small fortress around the temple and set up markets next to it. He then dedicated all his land in Sadri and his fortress on the Kankhal hills to the gods and named his kingdom Devlagarh – Castle of the Gods. No Rana would dare to attack a castle of the gods – such a sin would mean sixty thousand years in hell.

Surajmull lived safe and secure in Devlagarh, beyond the borders of all the other kingdoms, and died in peace. Thus was the yogini's prophecy fulfilled for him.

Jaimull and Surajmull were both now gone from Prithviraj's path to the throne of Mewar. The only one who remained was Sanga. One day, a spy brought news of Sanga to Prithviraj at the fortress of Kamalmeer. Sanga was alive and preparations were on for his wedding to the daughter of the king of Srinagar. Prithviraj immediately called his trusted advisers and sat down to plot how he could trap Sanga in his net.

But the forces that guided Prithviraj's destiny had not been sitting idle. Through night and day, light and dark, and in times of joy and grief, they had been relentlessly spinning a web that would ultimately ensnare Prithviraj. That web was now complete. As he was preparing to leave to catch Sanga, he received a letter from his sister, who was married to the king of Sirohi.

Her story appalled and enraged Prithviraj. She had written that her husband had been humiliating her, beating her and threatening to throw her out right from the day of their wedding. He was a drug addict and a lout. Her father was now an old man, so she was beseeching her brother to come and avenge the crimes against her and save her from certain death.

Prithviraj had set his horse's head towards Srinagar. But the moment he finished reading his sister's tear-stained letter, he turned around and set off for Sirohi. Fate had sent him riding in a direction absolutely opposite to where Sanga was, going further away from him with every hoofbeat.

It was night. The Maharana's daughter sat in her dark bedroom on the golden bed that her father had gifted her on her wedding, weeping, while her husband, the drug addict king of Sirohi, snored away. Prithviraj smashed the doors open and came in. He kicked the king out of his bed and held him by his throat. His sister caught Prithviraj's hand and pleaded: 'Please stop, please don't kill him.'

Prithviraj stepped back, but his fury had hardly abated. 'This man has the gall to lay a hand on you,' he said. 'He doesn't know that you are the Maharana's daughter? He needs to be whipped like a dog so that he knows what's what.'

By this time the king of Sirohi was absolutely sober and the haze of the drugs he had taken was all gone. He fell at Prithviraj's feet and begged: 'I'll never do it again. Please forgive me.'

Prithviraj grabbed him by the neck and stood him up. 'Take my sister's shoes, place them on your head and ask her for forgiveness,' he said. 'Only when you do that will I let you live.'

'You could have said that earlier!' replied the wretch. He quickly picked up his wife's shoes and put them on his head. And she said: 'Let it be for now. Go and give my brother some food and calm him down. Let me sleep a bit.'

The king of Sirohi, son-in-law of the Maharana of Chittor, sat Prithviraj down and plied him with the delicacies of his land, all of it served on plates of gold. Prithviraj had his fill – four or five of the laddoos whose secret recipe only the people of Sirohi knew, and a full jug of water. He then set off for Kamalmeer where his men were waiting for him.

But he would never reach Kamalmeer. The king of Sirohi had mixed the deadliest of poisons into the laddoos that he had eaten, to avenge the shame he had gone through, of having to place his wife's slippers on his head.

The sun was about to rise and the hazy outlines of the castle of Kamalmeer were already visible when Prithviraj fell from his horse on the dust of the roadside. The last sight he saw was of Kamalmeer, where his wife Tarabai was alone and waiting for him.

And then he was dead, his life force soaring through the fiery morning light to take the route of comets in the sky.

As Prithviraj fell dead, the musicians in faraway Srinagar were beginning to play the morning melody, '*Bhor bhayee* . . . Dawn has come . . .'

The one-eyed Sanga, or Sangramsingh, would be the next Maharana of Mewar.

Afterword

Rana Sanga or Sangramsingh would go on to build Mewar's largest empire. But nineteen years after his coronation, in 1527, he would be defeated by the invading Babur on the fields of Khanwa. Sanga was the most powerful king that Babur had to fight in Bharat.

In the battle of Panipat the year before, Babur had won against the Lodhis, who ruled from Delhi, but their kingdom was already quite weak. In fact, Rana Sanga had won every battle he had fought against the Lodhis and captured much of their territory. When Babur arrived, Sanga's kingdom stretched from most of Rajasthan through parts of what we today know as Gujarat and Madhya Pradesh up to the gates of Agra.

It is the battle of Khanwa, where Babur faced a united Rajput federation army led by Rana Sanga, that marks the true beginning of the Mughal era.

Ten months after Khanwa, Sanga was poisoned to

death by his own noblemen who did not want another war with Babur, a war that Sanga was preparing for, even though he had lost an eye, an arm and a leg in the many battles he had fought over the years.

It would be several decades before the Mughals would again face a serious threat from the Rajputs of Mewar, this time led by one of Rana Sanga's grandsons, Rana Pratap.

A Note on the Author

Abanindranath Tagore (1871–1951) was one of India's most important artists and led the influential Bengal School of Art. A member of the Tagore family, he was also a well-regarded writer, especially known for his children's books which includes the classic *Raj Kahini*.

A Note on the Translator

Sandipan Deb became a published author at the age of eight when one of his stories was printed in *Sandesh*, the Bangla children's magazine edited by Satyajit Ray. Since then his writings have ranged from business to cricket, cinema to artificial intelligence. He has been editor of the *Financial Express*, managing editor of *Outlook*, and founding editor of *Outlook Money*, *Open* and *Swarajya* magazines. An IIT-IIM alumnus, he is the author of several books, including *The IITians: The Story of an Extraordinary Indian Institution and How Its Alumni Are Reshaping the World*, *Fallen Angel: The Making and Unmaking of Rajat Gupta* and *The Last War*, a reimagining of the Mahabharata.